## Conquer Physical Pain

How would you like to be able to relax in a dentist's chair and virtually "will" away feelings of pain. Or stop smoking once and for all—without discomfort or withdrawal symptoms?

## *It Can Be Done*

Allergies, headaches, aches and pains, insomnia, overweight, compulsive habits—all of these can be caused by hidden influences from the subconscious mind. Reach that mind, and you can achieve a degree of self-mastery you never thought possible.

## *The Methods Are Safe and Simple*

*Self Hypnotism* shows you step-by-step exactly how to enter an hypnotic state, how to give yourself suggestions and make them work, how to set up a program for self-improvement, and even how to get information from your inner mind—while fully awake.

*As used by countless physicians, the ancient science of self hypnosis provides a much needed shortcut to a saner, healthier, happier life.*

# SIGNET Books of Special Interest

# Self Hypnotism

*The Technique and Its Use in Daily Living*

## LESLIE M. LECRON

**A SIGNET BOOK** from

**NEW AMERICAN LIBRARY**

TIMES MIRROR

Library of Congress Catalog Card Number: 64-10742

This is an authorized reprint of a hardcover edition published by Prentice-Hall, Inc.

SIGNET, SIGNET CLASSICS, MENTOR, PLUME AND MERIDIAN BOOKS
are published by The New American Library, Inc.,
1301 Avenue of the Americas, New York, New York 10019

FIRST PRINTING, FEBRUARY, 1970

12  13  14  15

PRINTED IN THE UNITED STATES OF AMERICA

*To my wife Lyn*

# *Foreword*

Leslie LeCron is by no means a beginner in the field of hypnosis. He is considered, and rightfully so, an established and highly qualified authority on the subject. He has written several other books of a more technical nature, books which are now being used by those working in the field of hypnosis. He is the editor of an excellent book entitled *Experimental Hypnosis,* and he has served as a pioneer lecturer and director of Hypnosis Symposiums, an organization which teaches the techniques of hypnosis to various professional groups throughout the country.

Having had the opportunity of listening to his lecture courses, I welcome the privilege of expressing my personal comments here. It is gratifying to know that Mr. LeCron has written a book that will not only benefit the health of many thousands of people but will also enlighten physicians, dentists, psychologists and other professional people regarding the inestimable value of hypnosis and auto-hypnosis.

Today, more than ever, people are seeking ways of helping themselves. They want to know how they can enjoy better health, achieve equanimity or peace of mind, and how they can become successful in life. Mr. LeCron proves to his readers that they can attain these goals via RIGHT THINKING. Because we are all susceptible to being influenced by our own thoughts, after we have mastered his techniques, we are free to do many new and wonderful things. This book makes possible the understanding of our inner selves. It utilizes the power of our subconscious minds, teaches us how to develop body-mind relaxation and inspires confidence in our individual potentialities.

Self-help, as the author points out, has many advantages over other forms of therapy. It is based on the premise that self-knowledge leads to self-confidence which in turn leads

vii

to effective self-discipline and ultimately results in a happier and healthier way of life.

Mr. LeCron's formula for successful living can best be summarized in his own words:

> Exploring the inner mind is the key to knowing yourself. It will unlock the door to the reasons for character and behavior problems, for emotional disturbances and illnesses, for traits such as phobias and fears and anxiety, and for many other personal problems such as everyone has. When you know the motivations and reasons behind these things, it is far easier to solve or overcome them and to make the changes which will bring health, happiness and success.

As a practicing psychiatrist I can vouch for the many benefits which patients derive from self-suggestion therapy. No one denies that certain conditions require the help of a specialist. But there are many things a person can do, with proper guidance, that will enable him to help himself. A book, such as this one, that helps people help themselves, is very much needed. People need to know more about emotionally induced illness. They need to know how to manage their emotions successfully, how to develop personality-maturity and cultivate a better sense of values.

This book achieves these very objectives. It teaches the reader the techniques of utilizing the power of his own mind for self-improvement.

FRANK S. CAPRIO, M.D.

# *Acknowledgments*

Acknowledgment is herewith made to the publishers for permission to quote or abstract from the following books:

Julian Press for quotations from my book *Techniques of Hypnotherapy*, including an article by Wayne Zimmerman, M.D.; also from *Origins of Illness and Anxiety* by J. A. Winters, M.D.

G. P. Putnam's Sons, Inc., from *Mobilizing The Mid-brain*, by Frederick Pierce.

Huna Research Publications, from *Self Suggestion*, by Max Freedom Long.

Farrar, Straus & Cudahy, Inc., from *Conditioned Reflex Therapy*, by Andrew Salter.

Stanford University Press, from *Psychotherapy by Reciprocal Inhibition*, by Joseph Wolpe, M.D.

Prentice-Hall, Inc., from *Autoconditioning*, by Hornell Hart.

# Contents

# Contents

# Contents

# Introduction

A number of books have been written offering ways for self-improvement and methods for overcoming emotional difficulties. The approaches taken by these books have ranged from positive thinking to self-hypnosis, from a completely materialistic point of view to the religious or metaphysical outlook. Many of these books have offered advice and techniques of definite value. Some people who have read them undoubtedly have used the methods and found them helpful. Other people probably purchased the books intending to use them but did not take the trouble, particularly when they discovered fhe methods complicated and time-consuming.

In general, the methods set forth by the authors of these books attempt to guide the reader in changing his way of thinking and in influencing the subconscious part of his mind. But most of these self-help books fail to consider one essential point: they fail to tell how unfavorable conditions develop and to explain what causes these conditions.

**You must know the source of the problem.** In order to improve yourself it is of utmost importance to find out the source of your problems. You must investigate character traits and behavior patterns. You must consider the possibility of emotionally produced illnesses.

A direct path to the inner mind, with insight into origins and causes of all personal problems, is the only real key to overcoming psychological difficulties and to changing your patterns of thinking and behavior. You will find such a key offered here, a rather unique and interesting one—*the crystal pendulum*. Its results are so astounding you will think this pendulum almost magical. Yet this technique has been used by hundreds of physicians, including a number of psychiatrists, and it is a proven new approach to uncovering origins and causes quickly and easily. By using it, you have the power to change your whole life.

Reading these pages will give you a better understanding of the way the subconscious part of the mind "works," how it affects you. You will learn how to contact the subconscious directly and how to influence it for your own self-improvement.

**Can you treat yourself?** But a question arises. Is the emotionally disturbed person, or one suffering from some personal problem or illness, able to help himself? Or must he depend on professional treatment? If you have a psychologically or emotionally caused illness, should you attempt to treat yourself? Of course, there are some conditions too deep-seated and too severe to be relieved without professional aid. However, there are many, many other symptoms and conditions where self-help methods can be applied, where it may even be easy to get well or clear up problems and wrong-thinking patterns through self-treatment. This is true whether the difficulties are emotional ones, harmful traits or habits, or, as stated above, even psychosomatic ailments. Too often, with the latter, a physician will treat only the symptom and not the cause. Drugs rarely will remove the causes which are buried deep within the inner mind.

**Everyone has some quirks.** Conflict and stress are among the more usual causes of tension. Under modern living conditions is anyone completely free of tension and stress? It has even been said that there is no such thing as a "normal" person. We all have some quirks. We all show illogical and compulsive behavior at times and suffer from emotionally produced diseases. Even a common cold may be psychologically caused.

Usually these difficulties are centered in the subconscious part of the mind. Seldom do we have conscious knowledge of their causes, but the inner mind knows all about them. The combination of conscious understanding of causes with the self-help methods of what to do about them as described in this book can remedy matters.

Early chapters tell you about the inner part of the mind, its make-up and the way it works; why we behave at times in a harmful, irrational way, and why emotional illnesses develop. You are provided with several methods for learning directly from your subconscious the reasons why you "tick" the way you do. Later chapters give methods of self-treatment to overcome such conditions and to change your wrong habits of thinking and behaving.

**Advantages of self-help methods.** Anyone with problems quite naturally wishes to be rid of them as quickly as possible—at once, not next year. Sometimes milder conditions can be corrected in a very short time; others may take longer. It is to be expected that treatment by a competent psychotherapist, a clinical psychologist, a psychiatrist, or a physician who practices psychosomatic medicine would often require less time than self-help. However, the expense involved, the difficulty in some localities of finding such a therapist, a record of previous failures in treatment, a situation where conditions are not too serious, and still other reasons may make self-treatment desirable.

**Set your goals and reach them.** If you wish to benefit yourself, a general knowledge of the usual sources of disturbance and illness is not enough. You must know which ones apply to your own particular condition. Generalities must be narrowed down to specific causes. Those which don't apply can be discarded. You must learn the ones which do affect you. These causes are seldom consciously known; your task is, therefore, to bring them into conscious awareness. The end result will be worthwhile. You will be able to *live* rather than merely to *exist*. Success will come in a surprisingly short time for many who employ these self-betterment methods. Health and happiness and success are everyone's goals and they can be reached through your own efforts.

**Use the whole book.** Some of the chapters about specific illnesses may not seem to concern you directly. Nevertheless, these chapters should be read because the matters mentioned will frequently apply to other conditions. Some of the possible causes for headaches may be the same as those producing arthritis or other ailments.

Many case histories are given which will help you learn how to gain from the subconscious part of your mind information you do not know consciously.

At the temple of Apollo at Delphos there is an ancient inscription—"Know Thyself." The real key to health and happiness and success is self-knowledge.

LESLIE M. LECRON

# Chapter 1

# WHAT YOU SHOULD KNOW
# ABOUT YOUR SUBCONSCIOUS

In your program for self-betterment you should know something about the make-up of the mind and the way it works, particularly about the inner part of the mind. It is from this inner mind that our difficulties come. You will learn how to influence it, how to learn the causes of the conditions you would like to change or overcome. It can best be influenced through hypnosis. You will learn about hypnosis and how to use autohypnosis in the next chapters.

**The make-up of the inner mind.** Almost everyone knows there is an inner part of the mind. It has been called "subliminal," "subjective," the "id," and by various other terms. In psychiatry the most commonly accepted designation is the "unconscious" mind. But unconscious has two meanings, the inner mind being one. It also means a period of unconsciousness, such as when a person is asleep, under an anesthetic drug, or knocked out as with a blow. Here the word "subconscious" will be used as most descriptive and preferable.

Most unfortunately we still know little about the actual make-up of this part of the mind or of the way it works. Even the ancient Greek physicians Hippocrates and Aesculapius were aware of there being such a part of our mental make-up. In modern times Sigmund Freud advanced our knowledge tremendously with his research into subconscious processes and with his psychoanalytic concepts. Since his day further research regarding the subconscious mind has been slight. This is most remarkable for it is recognized that much illness is emotionally or psychologically caused. Estimates vary as to the amount or percentages. Some physicians believe that about half of all illness falls into this category. Others have claimed as much as 80 per cent. A leading Canadian authority, Dr. Hans Selye, believes stress to be involved in generating all illness, even including infectious diseases, for stress lowers resistances so we become open to infections.

In the United States and to a somewhat less extent in other English-speaking countries, Freudian ideas are taught in all medical schools and other psychiatric training centers. Hence most psychiatrists accept them. In all other parts of the world Freud has had small acceptance and psychiatry is based on the work and theories of the Russian physiologist Pavlov. These theories will be described later.

The Freudian view of the make-up of the inner mind is undoubtedly correct in some respects, but it fails to account for all its operations and, on the whole, describes it in too mechanical a fashion. Freud did give us a much better understanding of some of the ways it operates. He believed that the mind as a whole consists of three main divisions. Our awareness, the part with which we think and reason, he called the *ego*. Another part, best thought of as the conscious, he termed the *superego*. Below consciousness is a part which he called the *id*, this being the seat of memory and of our basic instincts. Later Freud theorized as to a fourth part lying between the id and the ego, just below the level of consciousness, calling it the *preconscious*. The term subconscious as used in this book would include Freud's id, preconscious and superego.

Dr. Carl Jung, famous Swiss psychiatrist, believed that the superego is not just conscious but is the most spiritual part of the mind. He termed it the *superconscious* mind. Jung believed it to be a part of a universal subconscious, directly connected with God, or a part of the Supreme Being. This idea was adopted from some of the Oriental philosophies.

**Automatic writing.** There are still other ideas about the make-up of the inner part of the mind. The late Anita Mühl, a leading woman psychiatrist, experimented with automatic writing in trying to learn more about it. Automatic writing is a fascinating matter. If you hold a pen or soft pencil in the hand, the subconscious can control the muscles of your hand and write intelligibly without your being aware of what is being written. You can read a book or magazine while the hand busily writes. Interestingly, a few "automats" have been able to read with the conscious mind while the right hand writes on some subject and the left hand at the same time writes about something entirely different. Three mental activities carried on at once! A Ouija board, for example, is similar to automatic writing.

Dr. Mühl claimed that four out of five people can learn to write automatically, although several hours of training may be needed. Others have found the percentage much less. Almost any good hypnotic subject can write automatically while in hypnosis. People who doodle are usually able to learn quickly, doodling being the same type of activity, and doodling may be quite meaningful if you could interpret it.

In experiments using fifty different subjects, Dr. Mühl was able to secure automatic writing from seven different levels of the subconscious, each identifying itself. These ranged, she reported, from a part corresponding to Jung's superconscious to the lowest level of the mind which often identified itself as "the old Nick" or "the Devil" in us. This seems to be a part containing our basic drives and instincts—our caveman attitudes.

**The subconscious as a mechanical computer.** Still another theory of the make-up of this inner part of the mind has been well described by Dr. Maxwell Maltz (*Psycho-cybernetics,* Prentice-Hall, Inc., Englewood Cliffs, New Jersey). Norbert Wiener was the first to advance the idea of cybernetics, which states that the subconscious works very much as does an electric computer, acting through the brain. It is purely mechanistic, although so complicated that the most elaborate computer would be a toy in comparison. This theory would seem to deny the ability of the subconscious to reason.

Some psychologists, the behaviorists, have denied the existence of a subconscious mind, believing that we are entirely controlled by our conditioning and what has happened to us—that all our behavior and thinking is purely mechanical. This concept no longer has acceptance by present-day psychologists. It is easily refuted by the fact that automatic writing can be produced, which definitely shows the existence of an inner part of the mind which thinks and reasons.

This can further be demonstrated by means of subconsciously controlled movements made as signals in response to questions worded so they can be answered *yes* or *no*, which will be described in a later chapter. This is something almost anyone can do and it is merely a variation of automatic writing. It has been said, and is undoubtedly true, that the subconscious mind reasons only deductively, while the conscious part reasons both inductively and deductively.

**The subconscious controls the mechanism of the body.** One of the duties of the inner mind is the control of the body mechanism, working through the brain. It is something like a thermostat. One part of the brain regulates the autonomic nervous system and through it controls every organ and gland. Probably the subconscious is able to control chemical and electrical reactions as well. Hypnotic experiments have been made which scientifically prove the control by the subconscious of many such mechanisms.

By hypnotic suggestion circulation of the blood can be controlled, heart beat slowed or speeded up, action of organs and glands changed, the rate of healing of a wound or injury greatly increased, body temperature lowered or raised. Many other body changes can be induced through hypnotic suggestion.

**How the subconscious thinks and reasons.** If we expect to influence the subconscious with the aim of self-benefit, it is important to understand the way it works. At times it seems to be somewhat childish and immature. It takes everything entirely literally. Often we do not say what we really mean. For instance, a commonly used phrase is "that makes me mad." We mean that we are angry, but we are actually saying that we have become insane.

When a person is in hypnosis, the subconscious seems to be nearer the surface, or sometimes may largely have taken over conscious thinking, as it does writing in automatic writing. If a person in the waking state is asked the question, "Would you tell me where you were born?" he will almost invariably answer by naming the place. He interprets the question as a desire to know the location and names it. In a fairly deep state of hypnosis, the person would reply by saying "yes" or more likely would merely nod. That is the correct literal answer. Yes, he is willing to tell you. It is a good example of how the subconscious takes things literally.

A possibly detrimental situation may arise from this literalness of the subconscious. We do not have to be in hypnosis to pick up ideas. Sometimes a physician, baffled at a failure to cure some illness, may say to his patient, "I am afraid you can't be helped. You will have to learn to live with this condition." What does this mean literally? It means that the patient will die if he loses the symptom! Such an interpretation could prevent the patient from ever getting well of losing the symptom. He might then die. Naturally the physician making such a remark did not mean it as it was taken.

As we grow up, learn and mature, our conscious viewpoints about many things undergo changes. The subconscious may also change its viewpoints, but more often will retain those of childhood. If something happened to you at the age of six, your subconscious is likely to continue to look at it with the viewpoint of a six-year-old. A childhood incident where one is frightened, perhaps by a snake, may develop into a phobia about snakes which will persist, causing the person to go into a panic at seeing a harmless garter snake. Consciously the person recognizes that some snakes are harmless, although repulsive. Even the picture of a snake could bring a panic reaction.

A part of your self-therapy will be to bring changes of subconscious viewpoint towards some of the things that have happened to you in the past.

**Guilt and self-punishment.** We all exhibit compulsive behavior at times, inspired by the subconscious. Usually this is not consciously recognized as compulsive unless it is quite illogical or unreasonable. Sometimes we may realize we are behaving compulsively and will wonder why. Some compulsions may be very harmful or may handicap us greatly.

One of my patients, a schoolteacher, spent three to four hours every day compulsively washing her hands. They were always raw from this continual scrubbing. She could not stop doing it, and had no idea why it seemed necessary. Of course the cause went back to something she had done with her hands about which she felt guilty. She was trying unsuccessfully to wash away the guilt. Shakespeare wrote of this in *Macbeth,* with Lady Macbeth washing her hands in this way and crying, "Out, out, damned spot!"

Strong guilt feelings may bring about a compulsion for self-punishment. The technical term for self-punishment is *masochism.* In large factories it has been found that 80 per cent of the accidents during work happen to only 20 per cent of the employees. This shows that they are

often subconsciously inspired and thus are intentional.
Everyone does things at times and has thoughts for which
he feels guilty. It is part of human nature. A very large
percentage of accidents stems from a subconscious need
for self-punishment.

This inner part of the mind seems to pay no attention
to end results, only to an immediate need. If a person has
a compulsively inspired bad accident, he may lose his
income for a time, may be under heavy medical and hospital expense, may be permanently crippled. He may even
be killed. If the accident was masochistic, he is not the
only one being punished. His entire family will also suffer.
But these end results are ignored by the subconscious.
Strangely, sometimes one part of the subconscious will
compel a person to do something wrong, another part,
the superconscious perhaps, then punishes him for doing
it.

**How memory works.** The inner mind is also the store-
house of memory. It would seem that we record every
perception when received much as if a motion picture
had been made with sound effects and even with all the
other senses registered, not only sight and hearing but
touch, smell and taste as well. Under hypnosis the picture
can be replayed.

Only a very small part of all the things that happen to
us are subject to conscious recall. Most people have very
few conscious memories of things occurring to them before the age of five years. Perhaps a few exciting or very
interesting events may be remembered. Now and then
there may be a very early memory, but often it is something we were told about long afterwards. We only think
it is a real memory. Nevertheless, everything that happens to us is there in our subconscious memory in the
greatest detail. We can forget consciously, but the subconscious never forgets. Much that we consciously forget
continues to affect us in many ways. Hypnosis can be
used to prove the extent of unconscious memory.

Very often emotional difficulties trace back to our
childhood conditioning, sometimes to traumatic (frightening or shocking) experiences. Frequently we repress the
memory of unpleasant experiences. We push them out of
the conscious mind because we do not want to think
about them. Then they can become lost to conscious recall. Yet they may fester in the subconscious and later
cause much trouble. Repressed in this way, we then have
no conscious knowledge of the cause of the trouble.

When memory begins is a nice question. Is it at a few months of age, a year or two years, or can there be even earlier memories? Some physicians familiar with hypnosis are convinced that there is in the subconscious an actual memory of being born. Some even believe there can be prenatal memories. Dr. Nandor Fodor wrote a book (*Search for the Beloved*, Hermitage Press, New York) trying to prove the existence of birth and prenatal memories through the interpretation and analysis of dreams.

A person under hypnosis may seem to remember the experience of being born and will tell details of what apparently happened. I am convinced that these are usually real memories; however, this is very difficult to prove scientifically. A hypnotized person may merely be fantasizing or remembering something which he has been told but has forgotten.

Recalling early or repressed memories may be of great help in relieving emotional difficulties, in creating character changes, and in overcoming psychosomatic illnesses. Ways of doing this will be discussed in later chapters.

**How the inner mind protects us.** An important duty of the inner mind is your protection. This part of the mind is always aware and functioning, whether you are awake or asleep. It is even aware when the conscious mind is "out" as from a blow or when under an anesthetic drug.

The mother of a baby may be sleeping soundly, but at the first whimper or cry from her child she will instantly awaken. Her subconscious has said, "Come on, wake up! Something may be wrong with the baby."

If you inadvertently touch something hot, your inner mind sends messages instantly to the muscles of your arm and you snatch your hand away before you can think and analyze the situation. In many other ways the subconscious is always alert to guard you from harm and danger. Yet, paradoxically, it can also cause illness, even self-destruction.

Our behavioral difficulties, character disorders and traits, neuroses and psychoses, and psychosomatic illnesses are all conditions involving the subconscious part of the mind. These conditions can be overcome by changes of both conscious and subconscious attitudes and viewpoints, changes effected by insight into the origins and causes of these conditions.

From the foregoing description, it might seem as if there is another person inside us. Of course this is not a proper concept. We have one mind, made up of different parts. The mind has been compared to an iceberg floating in the sea: the conscious part is above the water, the subconscious is that under the water—a very large part of the whole.

The total person is a unit, a mind and a body, each influencing the other. The whole individual must be considered in dealing with emotional disturbances. The inner mind works through the brain to control the body and to affect it.

## SUMMARY

You should now have a fairly good understanding of your mental make-up. You think and are aware with the conscious part of the whole mind. Under the surface of awareness is the subconscious and the superconscious. Little is known about either, though the latter is especially elusive.

From automatic writing, we know that the subconscious reasons, though it seems to reason rather immaturely in some ways. It takes everything literally; it often retains childhood viewpoints and in self-therapy these may need to be changed. It has control of the entire body mechanism and in some illnesses this ability may be used for recovery. It never forgets and everything that happens to us is in our memory, though only a small amount can be consciously remembered. In hypnosis, memories of forgotten past experiences can be recalled. The subconscious may punish you at times for things you have done; yet one of its duties is to act to protect you from harm.

# Chapter 2

# HOW YOU CAN
# COMMUNICATE DIRECTLY
# WITH YOUR "INNER MIND"

In the program for self-betterment which you will be following, what you have learned of the subconscious will be used so that you can influence it, find out the reasons for detrimental behavior patterns and the causes of conditions which you wish to change or eliminate. You can affect your subconscious so you will be able to put it to work for you and take advantage of some of its remarkable abilities.

Insight into the causes or reasons for a condition is one of the principal goals in making changes. There are a number of ways of finding out these causes.

**What about psychoanalysis?** In psychoanalysis the main techniques used to gain such insight are free association and interpretation of such dreams as a patient may have. Free association is the term for the verbalization of all one's thoughts. The patient says whatever comes to mind, no matter what it is or how ashamed he might be of it. He is told it is important to hold nothing back. What may seem to him to be of slight consequence may be of great importance.

It is not easy to learn to speak so freely. It usually takes some time for a person to be able to tell everything that comes to mind. Some find it impossible. Naturally there is much waste of time, for our thoughts may be about completely unimportant matters. We tend to repress unpleasant things. The patient may block and be unable to bring out anything of value for session after session. Gradually he should, at least theoretically, reach the sources of troubles and with insight they should begin to disappear. When knowledge comes, there must also be a kind of digestive process and a change of subconscious viewpoint.

Dreams often give important clues to problems. Understanding the real meaning may be easy if the dream is not too complicated and full of obscure symbolism. More often, considerable knowledge and skill are required in order to understand the meaning of a dream.

For this purpose popular dream books are completely worthless and full of nonsense. Psychiatric texts can be read which teach proper dream interpretation. They will be found to be fascinating reading. In planning self-therapy it would be helpful to study one of these books if you are willing to take the necessary time, though it is by no means necessary. Probably the best texts are Gutheil's *Handbook of Dream Analysis* (Liveright, New York), and Fodor's *New Approaches to Dream Interpretation* (Citadel Press, New York). A popular paperback edition of Gutheil's book has been published but unfortunately is now out of print.

Psychoanalysis can be a successful method of treatment but the time involved is so long and costs are so great that it is a matter only for the wealthy. It is difficult to find accurate statistics as to results, but those published show it to be effective with only about one person out of four.

Other techniques are faster and give far better results. Hypnoanalysis is where analytic methods are used but with the patient under hypnosis. The same goals are reached in far less time. Other techniques with hypnosis are still more rapid and better in result.

**More about automatic writing.** Probably the ideal way of gaining information from the subconscious mind is by means of automatic writing. It should be realized that the subconscious knows just what is causing our emotional difficulties and our psychosomatic illnesses. This is the information we seek. With automatic writing, questions can be asked of the subconscious mind and replies written out. It may even volunteer information at times. However, repressions may prevent our learning the desired information.

Automatic writing is a fascinating phenomenon. With it, words are usually run together without spacing. The writing may be clear, but sometimes the letters are not well formed so it may be hard to read. It may be done very slowly, though sometimes the hand will race across the paper. The writing may be in the normal way from left to right but sometimes it will be backwards, upside down, mirror writing, or even a combination of all these ways. Often there is condensation. The word *before* might be written b4; the figure 2 used instead of any of the three ways of spelling the word. Why bother with extra letters?

**Other ways of communicating directly with your inner mind.** Since automatic writing is not always possible or feasible in terms of time, a variation is available which almost anyone can do readily. This involves setting up a code of communication by means of subconsciously controlled signals. Technically these are called *ideomotor* responses. Questions must be worded so they can be answered *yes* or *no* and the subconscious answers with signals. These consist of movements of an object which can be held so that it dangles and thus forms a pendulum.

**The pendulum method.** The pendulum may be any small light object such as a finger ring or an iron washer. A thread about eight or ten inches long is tied to this object. A ball made of lucite with a short chain attached can be purchased and makes an ideal pendulum. Some department stores sell a device called a "Magic Eye," which is a commercial adaptation of this means of communicating with the inner mind. As sold, it is supposed to be a method of predicting the future and is merely an adaptation of the Ouija board.

The pendulum has been used for hundreds of years as an attempt to foretell the future. Our use of it has nothing to do with prognosticating. It is merely a device for gaining information from the subconscious mind. It is by far the easiest and quickest way of learning the causes of emotional illnesses and other conditions.

This technique has been taught to several thousand physicians by a small group of physicians, dentists and psychologists known as Hypnosis Symposiums. It has been used in many thousands of cases to great advantage, its users including a number of psychiatrists.

In using the pendulum you should hold the thread or chain between the thumb and forefinger, with your elbow resting on the arm of your chair, or on a desk, or perhaps on your knee. The weight then dangles freely.

Four basic directions of movement of the pendulum are possible. These are a clockwise circle, counter-clockwise circle, back and forth across in front of you or in and out away from you. The inner mind can be asked to make its own selection of movements. One is to signify *yes*, another *no*. A third should mean *I don't know*, and the fourth *I do not want to answer the question*. This last may indicate resistance and is therefore important.

You may specify the meaning of each movement, but it is better to let the subconscious make its own selections. This seems to bring better cooperation on its part. It also shows you that the subconscious does think and reason.

Holding the pendulum, you should voluntarily move it in each of the four directions, then hold it motionless and ask which is to mean *yes*. In doing this no words are usually necessary. You merely think the request. The subconscious is asked to select any of the four motions which is then to represent an affirmative reply. You might word your request this way—"My subconscious is to select one of these four motions of this pendulum to mean *yes* in answer to questions." The pendulum will work better if you watch it.

Usually it will start to move within a few seconds, but sometimes it may take a moment or so "to warm up the motor." If it does not start to swing very quickly, think the word *yes* to yourself several times. Be sure you do not move the pendulum voluntarily. Try to hold it still, but you will find it will move of its own accord. If you still find there is no movement, have someone else ask the questions to establish the four movements for reply.

When your affirmative response has been set up, ask for selection of another motion to mean *no*, then for one of the two remaining ones to mean *I don't know*. The fourth will then represent not wanting to answer.

Probably you will find this very interesting. Many people exclaim in surprise as the pendulum swings in answering. Movements may be somewhat slight, but usually the arc of the swing is long and very definite.

There is nothing magical in this. It merely shows to the most skeptical that the inner mind does think and reason, and also that it is able to control muscular movements. The subconscious continually controls such movements. As you read this it is controlling your breathing muscles. When you walk you do not think of all the

# Chevreul Pendulum

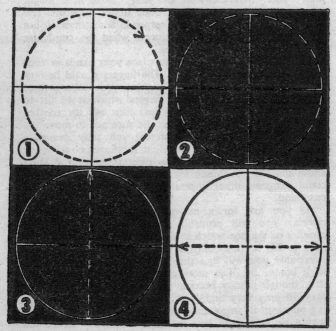

movements involved and the necessary coordination, although you had to learn these as a child. After you had practiced a bit, had fallen many times, you set up a conditioned reflex and your subconscious took over control of all the muscles involved. Your movements in walking then became involuntary. The same is true in learning to typewrite. Your typing would be very slow if you had to think consciously of the typewriter keys and how to strike them.

Almost everyone will find that the pendulum will move for them. If it does not for you, it is almost certainly a sign of resistance. Your subconcious may feel that you wish to learn something from it which it is not ready to let you know.

**Finger movements.** A similar means of questioning the inner mind is by means of replies made by movements of the fingers with involuntary control. This may be somewhat harder to accomplish and may take a little longer when you are awake. If it is done under hypnosis, few will find their fingers do not respond. Sometimes replies may be made by finger movements when the pendulum will not respond, and vice versa.

To establish finger movements place your hands in your lap or on the arms of a chair. The fingers should be outstretched and free to move. Then ask your subconscious to select any one of the ten fingers which is to lift to represent *yes.* When one has lifted then ask for another to lift to mean *no,* and so forth. Be sure not to move the fingers voluntarily. If you prefer, you may designate which finger is to move. The right forefinger could mean *yes,* the left forefinger *no;* the right thumb for *I don't know* and the left thumb for not wanting to answer. You could designate other fingers as you wish, perhaps all on one hand.

As you ask for a movement, observe your fingers closely. You will probably feel a slight tingle in the muscles of the one which is about to move, as the muscles start to lift it. It should rise towards a pointing position. Invariably you will find that it trembles or wiggles a bit as it comes up. The movement usually is quite slow at first, though it may become more rapid with practice. It may lift only very slightly or may rise to a straight pointing position. In using either the pendulum or finger movements be very sure you make no voluntary effort and when you are asking questions you should avoid consciously guessing what the answer will be.

**How to question your subconscious mind.** Wording
your questions properly requires some skill and knowledge. You will learn more about this from the case histories which will be given and from the discussions about
certain conditions. The questions must be clear, not vague
or ambiguous. Remember, the subconscious takes everything literally. Questions must be worded so you are
saying what you really mean.

When replies are made to some questions you may be
surprised to find the pendulum swinging at a diagonal,
or some other finger than those designated may move.
Here your subconscious is trying to tell you something.
It may mean *perhaps* or *maybe*. It may indicate that your
question is not clear or can't be answered properly.

When using this technique in self-therapy, it is best to
write out the questions you wish to ask, being sure they
are clear and properly worded. Then note the answers as
you receive them. Besides use in self-therapy, you may
find it helpful to get other information from your subconscious. If you must make a decision about some matter, the inner part of your mind has access to much more
data in your memory than you have consciously. It may
tell you which procedure would be best for you to follow.

Sometimes if you believe your intuition is working and
you have a "hunch" about something, you can check it
with your subconscious. If you lose something and cannot
find it, questioning of your subconscious may locate it.
You will find still other uses as you become more familiar
with this means of communicating with your subconscious.

I would recommend by all means that you avoid trying
to obtain predictions from your subconscious. There is
some evidence that this part of the mind at times may
have some knowledge of the future, but this is not proven
scientifically. You probably would get answers to questions about the future, if your subconscious is cooperative
and wishes to please, but in all probability it would only
be guesswork or fantasy. Trying to find which horse will
win a race is likely to be expensive!

In my experience and that of many therapists who have
learned to use this ideomotor questioning technique, the
answers given are usually correct. With most people the
subconscious will not give false information but instead
will sometimes say it does not wish to answer. Some
people will lie compulsively and then misinformation
might be offered. Answers may be taken with a slight
grain of salt until they can be verified, but as a rule they

can be depended on. A person who is a pathological liar or who has set up a habit of frequent lying may find his subconscious undependable in answering, but this is very exceptional.

If you believe a wrong answer may have been given, it is well to re-word your question in some other way. Perhaps it has not been clear. In questioning patients, I have often found the pendulum or fingers answering affirmatively while the patient will verbally be saying the answer to that question is certainly *no*. Invariably the subconscious reply is the correct one.

Another use of this type of questioning is in dream interpretation. Even a skilled analyst is not always sure of the meaning of some complicated dream. Interpretation can be checked by questioning, for the subconscious produced the dream and knows its symbolism and inner meaning.

There are some diagnostic possibilities here, though they have not been explored scientifically to any extent. The inner mind certainly can tell whether or not some illness is purely organic and physical or if it has some emotional or psychological causes. It may be possible that it would know what organ or part of the body may be affected in some illness, but a physician using the questioning for diagnosis would certainly trust his medical knowledge instead of depending on the patient's subconscious knowledge. He might question in this way for verification in case of doubt. Some have done this and have found the answer given proved later to be correct.

A young woman patient complained to me one day that she was having much pain in the pelvic area. She had visited her physician the day before—a gynecologist. He had examined her to see if she might have a tubal pregnancy or if anything else was wrong but had found no reason for the pain. Today it was much worse.

She asked if pendulum answers might tell us anything about the cause of the pain, so some questions were asked. In replying to one as to whether there was a tubal pregnancy the answer was *yes*. I urged her to see the physician again that day as something certainly was causing the increase in pain. When he made a more thorough examination he found she did have a tubal pregnancy.

An interesting experiment has been made with a number of obstetricians and other physicians collaborating and reporting their results. Since the inner mind has so much knowledge, would that of a pregnant woman know the sex of the unborn child? Using the finger or pendulum responses, 402 women were questioned. Three hundred and sixty correctly predicted the sex of the child, including three sets of twins, where the fact of their being twins and their sex were both stated correctly. Among the errors, most of the women predicted the sex as being the one for which they had a preference. Probably wishful thinking entered and the replies were on a voluntary basis rather than unconsciously controlled.

If you are using this questioning technique with some other person it is usually possible to tell if the movements are being made consciously or if they are involuntary. With the pendulum, the hand or fingers may not seem to move at all, or any movement will be very slight, although of course there is some movement of the hand or the pendulum would hang motionless. If the person being questioned is consciously controlling the motion, the hand can be seen to move and the swing of the pendulum is more pronounced.

With finger movements, the answering finger invariably will tremble a bit and will lift slowly, sometimes taking some time before it begins to lift. With practice and experience the movement may be more rapid, but there will still be a wiggling effect. The finger may lift only a fraction of an inch, or may come up to a full pointing position, though slowly. When there is voluntary control, the movement is always smooth and very much more rapid, lifting higher. Observation will show you if the person you are questioning is voluntarily causing the movement. In this case caution him to let the movement be of its own accord.

In self-help practice you will sometimes be using auto-suggestion. For it to be effective the idea must be acceptable to this inner mind, or it will not be carried out. Questioning may show if the subconscious is willing to produce the result you wish.

**Some other "uncovering" methods.** There is still another way to obtain answers from the subconscious, though it is not as accurate because the conscious mind may affect the situation. This is to imagine, with the eyes closed, that you are looking at a blackboard. Then ask your question and request the subconscious to write the answer on the imaginary blackboard in white chalk. If you have a good imagination and can readily visualize in this way, answers can often be had. When it "works," it is a rapid method.

Another type of uncovering device is sometimes helpful. When there is trouble in locating some cause or reason for a condition, a suggestion may be given the subconscious which if carried out will bring the answer. On going to bed at night, with the eyes closed, suggest to yourself that sometime during the next day you will have a revelatory thought about your question—that you will suddenly find the answer in your mind and recognize it as the answer. The suggestion should be that at some time next day such a thought is suddenly to pop into your mind. You must be specific as to what it will be about. It may fail to come, of course, but frequently you will find the answer.

It should be recognized that the great majority of our thoughts spring from the subconscious expressly through the association of ideas. One thought prompts another. We can direct our thinking processes, but much bubbles up directly from the subconscious.

You will find in other chapters, from the case histories given, much more as to how to use questioning. You will learn the types of questions which you will want to ask yourself and how they should be worded. You certainly will find that working with the pendulum or finger answers is a fascinating matter. Exploration of the inner mind is the key to knowing yourself. It will unlock the door to the reasons for character and behavior problems, for emotional disturbances and illnesses, for phobias, fears and anxiety, and for many other personal problems. When you know the motivations and reasons behind these things, it is far easier to solve or overcome them and to make the changes which will bring health, happiness and success.

While a home-devised pendulum will be found quite satisfactory, the lucite ball type on a chain can be obtained from the manufacturer, The Wilshire Book Co., Div. X, 8721 Sunset Blvd., Hollywood 69, Calif. Two sizes are available, one at a dollar, a larger one at two dollars. The plastic ball has the added advantage of being an excellent object on which to fix attention in inducing autohypnosis.

**How to develop automatic writing.** Before beginning a program of self-help it would be a good idea to find out whether you can readily learn automatic writing. You may find you have a facility for it and it is worth a bit of time to find out. If you are a "doodler," you are likely to be able to write automatically. If you can, it will give you another access to your subconscious and will be a great help in your program.

It is best to sit in a comfortable chair without arms. Take a breadboard or a lapboard of some kind and lay it across your knees. Cut off a piece of paper from a roll of shelfpaper, so it will cover the entire board. If you develop as an "automat," you can use such a roll of paper, pulling out enough to cover the board, and as your writing covers the sheet, then pull out another section of the paper.

If you sit at a desk, your arm does not have as much freedom to move as when it rests on a lapboard across your knees. Use a very soft pencil or a ballpoint pen which writes heavily, such as a laundry marking pen. Instead of holding it in the normal writing position, take it between the thumb and forefinger. Hold straight up and down, with the point resting on the paper. Start at the top left of the sheet of paper.

Now tell your subconscious mind that you would like to have it control your hand and write about anything it would like as a subject. Write your name, holding the pen or pencil as described. Make a few circles and then return your hand to the upper left-hand edge of the board. Make no further voluntary movement. Some people find the hand will move almost at once. More often it may not move for several minutes. When it begins to move of its own accord it may merely make lines or geometric figures, as though it were warming up or practicing. Watch the hand closely and keep thinking that it is going to begin to move. You may find a tingling feeling in the muscles or you may find that you have rather lost track of the entire arm, as though it were no longer a part of you. If it writes, try not to anticipate the words as they come.

The handwriting will not be like your usual writing. The words probably will not be separated. Movements may be rather jerky. The hand may move very slowly or may race across the board. You can try shutting your eyes, if you like, which helps to keep you from knowing what is being written as the hand moves.

Keep trying for at least twenty minutes if the hand does not move sooner. You might even try a second time if there is failure. When you have learned autohypnosis, you may use this technique to get good results. If you cannot produce automatic writing, do not be discouraged. Probably no more than one person out of five can do so without much effort and practice.

## SUMMARY

In this chapter you have learned that you can communicate directly with your inner mind and obtain information from it. This can be done by asking questions and obtaining answers through movements of the pendulum, or the fingers, or seeing words written on a blackboard "in your mind's eye." You may even be able to develop automatic writing and with it gain more detailed information.

These techniques will be of the utmost advantage in understanding the conditions which you wish to change.

*Chapter 3*

# HYPNOSIS: A POWERFUL
# FORCE FOR GOOD

In your program for self-betterment you naturally wish to accomplish your goals as rapidly as possible. Self-hypnosis offers you a very definite shortcut, and results will come more quickly if you use it. You may have the usual misconceptions about it, but with a proper understanding and knowledge about it, you can utilize its many advantages. Hypnosis offers the easiest access to the subconscious part of the mind; through hypnosis the subconscious can most readily be influenced to bring about the changes you want.

**Popular misconceptions about hypnosis.** The public has many misconceptions about hypnosis, some of which are shared by physicians. Nevertheless, probably twenty to thirty thousand women in this country have gone through childbirth under hypnosis. In addition, there have been thousands of others who have had therapeutic treatment in which hypnotic techniques have been used. Unfortunately, however, the misconceptions are still prevalent and many who could benefit from hypnosis do not have its help.

Almost everyone has the idea that a hypnotized person becomes unconscious. Most of us have a normal fear or dislike of losing consciousness. Actually, a subject is always completely aware even in the deepest stages of hypnosis. He knows what he is saying and doing. There is never loss of consciousness while in hypnosis. There really is very little sensation other than a feeling of list-lessness or lethargy. You can move if you wish, but it seems to be too much trouble. Talking may require an effort due to the lethargy. There is so little other sensation that many who go only into a light state may think they have not been affected at all. This is quite usual.

When one is deeply hypnotized there is a recognition of it. Even in a medium state one feels that something is "different." The skillful operator tries to produce some hypnotic phenomena which will let his subject realize he is in hypnosis. The operator may suggest that the subject's eyes cannot be opened. The subject finds to his surprise that he cannot open them. Suggestions of extreme heaviness of an arm may prevent its movement when an effort is made to lift it. When such suggestions work, it shows the subject that he is in hypnosis. If awake, he would open his eyes or move his arm readily.

Another popular misconception is that the subject must carry out any suggestion given him. But the operator is not omnipotent and the subject is never "in his power." Hypnosis would be highly dangerous if the operator had such control. Thousands read books about hypnosis and learn how to induce it; some certainly would take advantage of having complete control of a subject. Newspapers would publish any news story about crimes or other bad uses of hypnosis. No one will do anything under hypnosis which would be against his principles nor will he carry out a suggestion unless it is acceptable. Fear of loss of control can prevent induction or hold the subject back from reaching deeper stages.

Another fear often entertained, but based on a mistaken idea, is that the hypnotized person might say something he would not want to talk about. Since there is complete awareness, the subject knows what he is saying. He would no more betray a "state secret" under hypnosis than he would when awake.

Somewhat along the same line is a belief in the inability to lie or give misinformation under hypnosis. If a person wished to be untruthful while hypnotized, he could readily lie.

A young man once brought his wife to me to be hypnotized so he could learn from her whether or not she had been unfaithful to him. He was intensely jealous and paranoid. He was informed that I would do this only if she was willing and that he could not be present while hypnosis was induced but could talk to her following induction. I told her alone that she did not need to comply with his urging and while hypnotized could answer him in any way she wished. The wife said she had nothing to conceal and was quite willing to be questioned under hypnosis. When he asked her about it, she denied any infidelity, which satisfied him, at least for the time being. His paranoid jealousy would probably lead to further suspicions later. His mistaken belief in her inability to lie under hypnosis aided in preserving their marriage, however.

"What if I should not wake up after being hypnotized?" is a question sometimes asked. This is an exceedingly rare occurrence, for a subject easily awakens on being told to do so. In fact, anyone can awaken himself at any time. In the few times when there is difficulty in awakening, there is always some motive or reason for it. Perhaps the subject is merely very comfortable and dislikes to leave his pleasant state of relaxation. If the operator went away and left a subject in hypnosis he would awaken whenever he wished to arouse himself.

What about dangers in hypnosis? Are there any dangers in hypnosis? An inexperienced operator who knows little about it might cause home trouble. He might forget to remove some suggestion he has given, such as forgetting to bring back sensitivity when hypnotic anesthesia has been induced. This might cause some difficulty, as a rule, however, suggestions would soon lose their effect in such a case. It certainly is foolish to permit an unqualified person to hypnotize you. Stage hypnotists, who seldom know much about it other than how to induce it quickly and to produce some phenomena would fall into this category. A physician, psychologist, or dentist with training in the use of hypnosis is aware of the few possible dangers and knows how to avoid them easily.

As to self-induction, thousands have learned it and I have yet to hear a report of any bad result from its use. The one precaution should be to remove any suggestion or phenomena before awakening yourself.

This book is not intended as a text on hypnosis. For the benefit of those who might wish to learn more details about it, the following list of primary texts may be helpful. There are scores of good modern books on the subject and only a few can be mentioned here. Most public libraries would have at least one of them.

LeCron and Bordeaux, *Hypnotism Today*, New York: Grune and Stratton.

Cooke and Van Vogt, *Hypnotism Handbook*, Los Angeles: Borden Publishing Co.

Estabrooks, *Hypnotism*, New York: Dutton.

Weitzenhoffer, *General Techniques of Hypnotism*, New York: Grune and Stratton.

**Why don't more physicians use hypnosis?** The question is sometimes asked as to why hypnosis is not used by more physicians and dentists. There are several reasons for this. Professional men usually have the same misconceptions as does the public. Many of them fear its use because of scare articles which have appeared in medical journals and popular magazines. Most of these have been written by psychiatrists who oppose the use of hypnosis except by psychiatrists. The American Psychiatric Association advocates the use of psychotherapy by general practitioners and medical specialists, and the AMA has made a similar recommendation.

One of the main reasons why it is not utilized more is the matter of the time needed. Thirty to forty (or more) minutes for hypnotherapy is usual. If a busy physician sees forty to fifty patients a day, he seldom can take this amount of time for an individual patient. Some production-line doctors see eighty or more patients a day! Scarcely enough time per patient for any good treatment.

Dr. David Cheek of San Francisco, a leading gynecologist with years of hypnotic experience, published an article in *Northwest Medicine* (February, 1962), pointing out the fears and woeful lack of knowledge about hypnosis in the medical profession, including the psychiatrists. He mentions a questionnaire sent out to 930 California psychiatrists about hypnosis. Only fifty reported ever using hypnosis as a technique and only twenty of the fifty said they found it of great value. Being acquainted with most of the twenty, I can add that they have found it of extremely great value.

Obviously something is wrong if only some two per cent find it valuable. Why is it extremely valuable for them and not for the other thirty who have used it? The only answer is that the others must not have enough knowledge about it and do not know how to use it effectively, or they, too, would find it valuable. This leaves the regrettable situation where almost 98 per cent of the California psychiatrists are ignoring something which obviously *is* of great value. Presumably these same percentages apply, more or less, to the entire United States. It is not so in Russia, where most psychiatrists use it.

Still another good reason for lack of professional interest is that physicians have had almost no opportunity to learn hypnotherapy, either while attending medical school or in post-graduate courses. Only three or four such courses in hypnosis have ever been offered by medical schools. Dental schools also have been negligent in this regard, though several have offered instruction.

Probably fifteen to eighteen thousand physicians, dentists and psychologists have had instructions in hypnotic techniques, but through privately given courses. In 1952 I felt there should be such courses given by a panel of instructors and organized such a group. We have offered some seventy-six symposiums teaching hypnosis to professional men. They have been given in various cities all over the United States, and also in Canada, Mexico and some Caribbean countries. Later, several similar groups were organized.

As a result of the interest aroused in this way, two national professional societies are now functioning, with a total of nearly four thousand members. Each publishes a quarterly technical journal about hypnosis. Their members are the leaders in the field, though there are others actively using hypnosis who do not belong to the societies. Some who have taken classes use it not at all or infrequently because of some of the reasons outlined above.

So that any interested reader may locate a physician, psychologist, psychiatrist or dentist who does use hypnosis and who practices in the reader's area, the names and addresses of these national societies are given. By writing them, being sure to enclose a stamped, self-addressed envelope, a qualified practitioner can be located. They are:

The Society for Clinical and Experimental Hypnosis, 353 W. 57th St., New York, N.Y.

The American Society for Clinical Hypnosis, 800 Washington Ave., S.E., Minneapolis, Minn.

**Some of the characteristics of hypnosis.** The depth a person reaches in hypnosis is usually classed as a light state, a medium one, or a deep state. In light hypnosis the following symptoms or phenomena can usually be produced or will be shown—relaxation with a tendency

not to move, a fluttering of the eyelids when closed, inability to open them on suggestions to that effect, hand-
clasp test, listlessness, a feeling of heaviness particularly
in the arms and legs, limb catalepsy (extreme rigidity or
looseness of the muscles of the limbs, with a tendency
for them to stay in any position in which they are placed),
and a partial type of age regression. Some of the phenomena mentioned will be explained later.

For the medium depth of trance—complete body catalepsy, anesthesia of any part of the body, either partial
or complete, greater relaxation, partial amnesia on awakening if suggested, greater lassitude, control of some
organic functions such as bleeding and salivation.

In deep hypnosis—complete age regression, ability to
open the eyes without awakening (possible often in a
medium trance), complete anesthesia, complete amnesia,
control of body functions, positive or negative hallucina-
tions of all five senses, time distortion.

There are other symptoms and phenomena but these
are the main ones. There is rapport with the operator in
all stages. Posthypnotic suggestions can be effective at
any depth, although the deeper the trance the more likely
they are to be carried out. A posthypnotic suggestion is
one given in hypnosis which is to be executed after
awakening.

It is possible to tell how deep a person is in hypnosis
by observing symptoms, testing, or by questioning with
ideomotor responses, which will be described in the next
chapter. Certain things are characteristic of each of the
three stages of depth, as listed above, though individual
responses may vary. One individual might not produce
hypnotic anesthesia in a very deep state while another
might do so in only a light stage.

The most important phenomenon used in self-therapy
is partial age regression. This is the ability to return in
time to some past event or some certain age and to relive
it with all five of the senses. It is much more than merely
remembering something. Complete regression, sometimes
called revivification, is never actually complete, of course.
A deep state is required for this and it would be exceptional to be able to regress in this way with autohypnosis.
When an operator tells a subject he is now some certain
age, the subject seems to become that age with the complete type of regression. He will behave like a five-year-old
if told he is that age. The identity of the operator would
not be known to him. Life from the suggested age on

seems to be blotted out. Scientific research has shown such a regression to be valid, not a pretence.

The partial type of regression is easily obtained in only a very light state with most people. Here the subject will go back and seem to relive an experience just as it happened, with all five senses functioning, seeing, hearing, etc. But he is also aware of the operator's identity and of his own actual physical location. There is a kind of duality involved.

It is this type of regression which is best used in psychotherapy and in self-help. It is easy to invoke and the subject is able to analyze and understand what is happening to him during the regression. He will be able to understand how some past experience may be affecting him in his present life. With the complete form of regression there is no insight or understanding of this, because it is' viewed with the same viewpoint held at that time. With either type of regression events at a very early age may be brought out which cannot otherwise be recalled. Examples of how regression is used will be given later.

**You've been self-hypnotized many times.** You have entered hypnosis spontaneously literally hundreds or even thousands of times, depending on your age. We all slip into a trance at times every day of our lives, though such situations are not labeled hypnosis.

Dr. Griffith Williams, of Rutgers University, has written of these spontaneous states in an article in *Experimental Hypnosis* (New York: Macmillan, LeCron editor). Daydreaming is nothing but a state of hypnosis, perhaps light, sometimes deep. When we concentrate intently on anything, such as reading a book, watching a motion picture or TV program, or even on our work, we tend to slip into a trance. It is even probable, as Estabrooks has pointed out, that we do so whenever we experience a strong emotion, such as fear or anger.

In any religious ceremony, particularly if there is music and ritual, many in the audience will enter hypnosis spontaneously. Almost anyone who drives a car will recall situations conducive to hypnosis—out on the open road, relaxed at the wheel, eyes fixed on the white line of the road, the monotonous hum of the motor, and you suddenly realize you have passed through some town and are beyond it but with no memory of having gone through it. You have been in hypnosis, experienced symptoms of amnesia, and then awakened yourself.

Awareness of these common spontaneous states which we all experience should relieve any fear or apprehension about being hypnotized or using autohypnosis. A trance state is quite a common, normal phenomenon.

## SUMMARY

In this chapter you have learned the facts about hypnosis. Properly used it is not dangerous and professional men trained in its use know how to avoid the few dangers. It is perfectly safe in every way to use self-hypnosis. While in hypnosis you are always fully aware and never "pass out" no matter how deeply you may go. You never lose control of yourself.

Thousands of professional men have been trained in the use of hypnosis and now use it in their practices. Names of some in your own locality can be obtained from one of the two national societies.

You have learned some of the interesting phenomena which can be produced with hypnosis in the three stages of depth. The common spontaneous states of hypnosis which we all enter daily are normal and knowledge of these should relieve you of any fears about it.

# Chapter 4

# SELF-HYPNOSIS GIVES YOU
# THE KEY TO A HAPPIER LIFE

Now that you know the facts about hypnosis you are ready to learn how you can hypnotize yourself for your own benefit. While in hypnosis you can influence and affect your subconscious mind more readily. You can put your inner mind to work for you.

Most people find self-hypnosis relatively easy to master. Some may find it difficult, others will find they succeed well on the first attempt. It will probably require practice, for a learning process is involved. It may take several attempts.

The easiest and quickest way to learn autohypnosis is to visit a physician or psychologist who uses hypnosis. One, two, or perhaps three sessions might be necessary. (Stay away from anyone who advertises himself as a hypnotist!) After induction by the therapist, you would be given posthypnotic suggestions for inducing the state yourself. Some brief formula to follow will be suggested, both as to entering and deepening hypnosis. You will be carrying out the posthypnotic suggestion when you follow the formula and will slip in readily. With a few practice sessions, you should quickly reach a good depth.

**How to induce self-hypnosis.** Lacking an opportunity to be hypnotized first by someone else, the following method will show you how to hypnotize yourself. For practice in self-induction, it is best at first to use some object for eye fixation. When you have become proficient this will not be necessary. Almost anything will do—a picture on the wall, a spot on the ceiling, anything at which you can look without discomfort. One of the best objects is a lighted candle placed in a saucer or holder where it can be watched comfortably. The flickering flame of the candle has a hypnotic effect. Watching a fire in a fireplace also is effective. The lucite ball pendulum is also an excellent object on which to concentrate. If you have a record player, you will find soft, slow music will be helpful.

A comfortable position should be taken, either sitting or lying down. As you watch the flame of the candle (or whatever), take three or four deep breaths to aid in relaxing. It is not necessary to say anything aloud; give yourself suggestions by thinking them.

One suggestion might be, "As I watch this candle my eyelids will become heavier and heavier. Soon they will be so heavy that they will close. Soon I will be in hypnosis." You can put this into your own words, repeating it several times as you watch the candle. As you feel your eyelids become heavier, let them close whenever you wish. A minute or two should be enough; prolonged staring is completely unnecessary.

As your eyes close, you should have a key word or phrase ready to serve as a signal to your subconscious to bring you into hypnosis. A good one is "relax now," though any will do. The "now" in this phrase is important because it means immediately, not sometime later. This phrase should be repeated slowly, three times.

You should then begin relaxation of your muscles. Start at your feet. Let the muscles of your right leg relax from the toes up to your hip; then the left, in the same way. Wiggle your toes and tighten all the muscles first, then let them go loose and limp. Then let the stomach and abdominal muscles relax, following with the chest and breathing muscles.

You will probably notice that your breathing becomes slower and more from the lower part of your lungs—abdominal breathing. Sometimes this speeds up at first, as does the pulse, as one goes into hypnosis. While sinking a little deeper both tend to slow down a bit.

Then let your back muscles relax, following with the shoulders and neck. Often we have a good deal of tension in this area. Continue with the arms, from the shoulders to the finger tips. As you go a little deeper, the facial muscles will also relax and loosen of their own accord.

One of the signs of hypnosis is a smoothing out of the facial muscles, with a lack of expression shown, a kind of woodenness of the features.

You are now ready to go deeper. Think to yourself, "Now I am going deeper and deeper," repeating it several times. Unless you dislike riding escalators, such as are in many department stores, imagine yourself standing at the top of one. In your mind's eye see the steps moving down in front of you and visualize the railings. Count backwards slowly from ten to zero, imagining as you start to count that you are stepping onto the escalator and standing with your hands on the railings while the steps move down carrying you with them deeper and deeper.

When you reach zero in your count, think of yourself as stepping off the escalator at the bottom. The first three times you practice self-induction, visualize yourself going down three different flights of the escalator, from floor to floor, counting each time as before. When you have become more proficient, going down only one level should be enough.

If you dislike riding escalators, as some women do, substitute an elevator or staircase. A patient once told me he did not like to go down and asked if he could go up instead. Why not? It makes no difference. Going down is associated with the idea of deeper. If you prefer to go up, avoid the words *deep* and *deeper* and substitute *far* and *farther* instead.

You should now be at least lightly in hypnosis. Some will find they have gone quite deeply by this time. More suggestions can be made of going still deeper, if you wish. To help in this you might then imagine yourself as being some place where you could relax well and enjoy it. This could be an imaginary scene—at a lake or on the sea, up in the mountains, fishing, boating, at home in your living room—anything pleasant. Concentrating on such an imaginary scene will tend to take you still deeper.

The beginner probably will be wondering if he is getting results. Your mental attitude should be positive rather than negative. In your early practice sessions do not care if you are having success. Practice will bring it. Be sure not to "try." Trying holds you back, while being passive and not caring will help. Take it for granted that you are at least lightly in hypnosis, as is probable.

**How to measure the depth of hypnosis.** A person in hypnosis does not remain at any given depth. There is a fluctuation. In a deep stage you may become aware of a kind of wave pattern. You tend to sink down into the trough of the wave, then to come up on the crest, very slowly. If you sense this, you undoubtedly have reached a good depth.

Hypnotic states are usually classed as light, medium or deep (deep is often termed somnambulism). You may wonder how deeply you have gone. In your first half-dozen practice sessions, pay no attention. Subsequently you can learn from your inner mind as to the depth you reach. If we give the subconscious a yardstick with which to measure, it can supply this information. It seems to have the ability to establish such a measurement quite accurately, as tests have shown. You can learn the depth by questioning your subconscious with ideometer replies.

A yardstick for the inner mind to use can be an imaginary yardstick of thirty-six inches. We can arbitrarily say that a light state is the first foot, one to twelve inches. A medium state is twelve to twenty-four inches, and a deep one is twenty-four to thirty-six inches. There is a still deeper stage which has been called a plenary trance, but for even an excellent subject to reach such a depth takes several hours of continued induction. Few are able to go so deeply and it is probably impossible with self-hypnosis. You may disregard this entirely. It has no advantage, except in research.

While you are in hypnosis you can find the depth by using finger responses to questions; after you have awakened you can use either the fingers or the pendulum to learn from your subconscious the depth you reached.

Questions can be worded something like this: "What is the deepest I have been today? Have I been as deep or deeper than twenty inches on my yardstick?" If the answer is *no* you should ask, "Have I been as deep as or deeper than fifteen inches?" If the first answer is *yes,* ask as to twenty-five inches. By bracketing in this way you can find the exact depth. You could narrow it down to a definite figure if you wish, but within five inches is enough for all practical purposes.

**Awakening yourself—relaxed and refreshed.** When you wish to awaken yourself, you need merely think, "Now I am going to wake up." Then count slowly to three, or to five if you prefer. You will find that you will always awaken relaxed, refreshed, feeling exceptionally well. However, it is well to give yourself a suggestion to that effect. Subjects have, on occasion, complained of a slight

headache on awakening. This is rare and the reason for
it is not apparent. Any possibility of this will be prevented
by such a suggestion.

While in hypnosis time may seem to pass very quickly.
You may find you have been in the trance for half an
hour when it has only seemed like a few moments. If you
are tired when you induce self-hypnosis, you may drop
off into a normal sleep. This can be prevented by suggestions of remaining in hypnosis until you awaken yourself. The length of time you wish to be in hypnosis can
be regulated. While looking at the candle, or before beginning the relaxation process, give yourself a suggestion
of awakening spontaneously after a given number of
minutes or at a certain time. You will then do so.

In a deep state there is considerable lethargy, both
physical and mental. It is too much trouble to move or
even to think very much. It may be hard to concentrate
your attention on whatever you may be trying to accomplish. Therefore, when giving yourself suggestions, it is
much better to go no deeper than a medium stage. Probably the ideal depth for most autohypnosis is from about
twenty to twenty-five inches on our yardstick. Much can
be accomplished even in a very light state; a medium one
is best.

When the idea has been offered to the subconscious
and repeated about three times, letting yourself sink a
bit deeper will permit the subconscious to register and
digest the suggestions more thoroughly. While it does this,
your mind should be diverted from whatever suggestions
have been made to something else.

**Practicing self-induction and testing the results.** In your
initial sessions of induction, allow about a half-hour or at
least twenty minutes for getting into hypnosis and deepening the stage. *For the first four or five attempts you should
not try to find out how deeply you have gone.* It might
be discouraging if you learned it was only a very light
stage or none at all. Each time you practice, you should
slip in a little deeper. After about eight or ten sessions
you probably will be reaching about as great a depth as
you can achieve, though this is not always so. After the
fifth session some tests may be made. Of course if you are
sure you are reaching quite a deep state after one or two
attempts you can proceed sooner with tests. When you
have succeeded with some of the tests, then you can begin
producing some of the interesting and often valuable
phenomena.

The first test should be what is called "hand levitation." Let your arms, resting beside you or on the arms of your chair, relax completely. (This is after you have hypnotized yourself.) Concentrate on your right arm, if you are right-handed; on the left if left-handed. You may be feeling a heaviness in your arms. Suggest to yourself that the heaviness will quickly disappear, imagine the weight of the arm draining out.

Then think, "My arm is getting lighter and lighter, lighter and lighter. All the weight is dwindling away. Soon it will be as light as a feather. My hand will begin to lift up into the air. The arm will bend at the elbow and the hand will float up, lifting up higher and higher. Soon my hand will touch my face."

As you make these suggestions, a feeling of lightness will gradually develop in the arm. Before the hand lifts, you may be aware of movements of the fingers, followed by the whole hand beginning to float upward. Keep repeating these suggestions. Be sure there is no voluntary effort made to lift the arm, but do not hold it back. It will move of its own accord, controlled by your subconscious mind.

The time needed for the hand to reach the face will vary considerably with different individuals. It may take several minutes, though rarely that long. When the arm first begins to lift, you will notice that it moves in little jerks, the movement being very slow. As the arm rises higher, the movement may become faster (you can suggest this) and with less jerkiness. When your hand has touched your face, let the arm fall into any comfortable position. If this test is successful, you can be sure you have reached a light state of hypnosis.

Try again in your next session if there is failure.

**The eyelids test and the hand-clasp test.** Another test may be made. While closing your eyelids tightly, suggest that you are going to count to three and will then be unable to open the lids. Repeat this with the thought, "The harder I try to open them, the tighter the lids will stick together." Then make your suggestions something like this: "One—my eyelids are glueing tightly together, glued fast together. Two—it's as though they were welded into one piece, welded together and I cannot open them. Three —now they are locked, locked tightly together."

Keep repeating the word *locked* again and again while you now try to open your eyes. If the test is successful, the lids will stay closed no matter how hard you try to open them. In accepting these suggestions, your subconscious blocks the nerve impulses from reaching the muscles of the eyelids so they do not move. The suggestions should be given slowly, allowing time for them to become effective. Don't rush it.

Another good test similar to this is called the handclasp test. It is done by clasping the hands together in front of you, or above your head with the palms turned out away from you. While you squeeze the fingers and knuckles tightly together you give the same suggestions as with the eyes but substitute hands for eyelids in the wording. If you are holding your hands in front of you, be sure to squeeze the palms tightly together.

**Suggestions for self-hypnosis.** When there is difficulty reaching hypnosis with the simple method given previously, a longer induction may be needed. More suggestions can be made, an actual induction talk can be employed. After you have repeated your key phrase three times, and before using the imaginary escalator, give yourself suggestions somewhat as follow:

"As I lie here comfortably, I will find myself relaxing more and more with each breath I take. My eyes are closed now and I will begin to feel a pleasant listlessness creep over me. I'll give way to this feeling. It is so pleasant to relax. My arms and legs will begin to feel heavy. I am drifting into hypnosis and relaxing more and more. It is as if all problems have been set aside and nothing seems to matter. I will feel a sense of comfort and wellbeing. Drifting deeper and deeper, deeper with every breath I take. As I count backwards and imagine the escalator (or elevator or staircase) I will go deeper with each count."

This induction talk may be memorized or changed into your own phrasing, keeping the ideas expressed in it. When you have said it to yourself, then use the escalator technique for further deepening.

When your early practice sessions have been completed and you begin making tests or suggesting phenomena, you will find that any successful test or production of phenomena tends to take you still deeper.

**Some uses of autohypnosis.** Self-hypnosis can be of great value in many ways. It is the best means available for overcoming insomnia. If you ever have such difficulty, put yourself into hypnosis on going to bed. Then you can suggest passing from hypnosis into natural sleep, wording it like this, "I will gradually relax more and more, becoming sleepier and sleepier. Within a few moments I will fall sound asleep and will sleep soundly all night long." After making such a suggestion, your mind should be diverted at once to anything pleasant, with no further thought of sleep. This is quite important—thinking about it tends to prevent your subconscious from producing sleep. A good night's rest should follow.

Insomnia is sometimes a deep-seated neurotic symptom. Suggestion may not overcome it, therefore, and you will need to uncover the causes. Methods for doing this for the insomnia case will be described later.

Self-hypnosis has many other advantages. You will find yourself more relaxed during your daily life. Hypnotic suggestion can inhibit fatigue. If you are tired at the end of the day and must go out that evening, a few moments in hypnosis, with suggestions of waking refreshed and rested, will bring back feelings of vigor and vitality.

When you have learned how to produce hypnotic anesthesia, there will be times when this ability will be of much help. Being able to shut off pain may be a real asset in visiting your dentist, or following a painful accident. However, pain has a purpose, and discretion and common sense must be used in turning it off. A pain in the abdomen might be a symptom of appendicitis, and to shut it off could be dangerous. People dying of cancer, in great pain, have been taught autohypnosis and so have been more comfortable in their last hours. Hypnotic anesthesia should only be used when it obviously is all right to stop the pain.

Self-hypnosis may be very helpful in studying and learning. If you are a good enough subject to be able to open your eyes and stay in hypnosis, you can study while in the trance. Concentration, ability to absorb new material, recall ability and examination performance are much improved under hypnosis.

When you intend to open your eyes while in hypnosis, a suggestion should be made that you will go even deeper as you open them. There is a tendency to awaken, or for the depth to lessen, on opening the eyes. Probably this is due to associating opening of the eyes with awakening, as we do from sleep.

HOW SELF-HYPNOSIS HELPED THE SCHOOLTEACHER. A schoolteacher who had returned to summer school to take up a course in plane geometry in order to earn her degree told me she was having great difficulty with the said course. She was halfway through the six-week term and said she hated the subject, did not understand it and could not force herself to study properly. She was an excellent subject, so I advised her to study under autohypnosis and to take her examination while in a trance. She followed the advice and received an excellent grade. Others have also found their grades increased with this method.

The main purpose of self-hypnosis is to influence the inner mind through suggestion. It will greatly shorten the time in reaching your goals in any program of self-therapy.

**How to use partial age regression.** In your self-help program you will sometimes need to use age regression. There should be no attempt to induce deep hypnosis in this respect, for you would then have no insight into the effect of past experiences. You can regress if only in a very light state of hypnosis. Your first effort should be to go back in time to some very recent and unimportant experience. *This is more than simple memory recall.* You should aim to relive an experience with all five senses functioning.

While in hypnosis, select as your goal the last meal you ate when someone was with you. Suppose it was breakfast with your wife present, as an example. Give yourself the suggestion, "I am now going back in time to my breakfast this morning and will relive the experience. I am drifting back in time, back in time to my breakfast this morning." Repeat this suggestion. Try now to visualize the situation. At first the scene may be a bit hazy. Then it will tend to clear and become more vivid.

Try to see the table in front of you and look at your wife. See what she is wearing; note the color and design of her clothes. Try to bring out other details as the scene becomes more vivid. Get a feeling of position. Feel the chair or seat under you.

Now go to the moment when you drank some coffee. Look at the cup; see its color; pick it up and feel it in your fingers. As you lift it to your mouth, smell the pleasing odor. Sip and taste the coffee.

After you have put the cup down, look at whatever food is before you and see it clearly as to color and shape. Then go to the moment when your wife spoke to you about something. Try to hear anything she may have said. You can actually hear her voice. Try particularly to develop the hearing sense, listening to whatever may have actually been said.

All of these things tend to turn mere memory into actual reliving of the incident. With a little practice you should readily learn to regress in this way to a recent experience. You will find yourself bringing out little details that could not be recalled if you were to rely on memory alone. If you find yourself unable to regress in this way, have someone else talk to you while you are in hypnosis. They can read over the suggestions above and then can tell you to do all these things as they have been written here.

During your next session you can learn to return to some childhood experience, perhaps one which has been completely forgotten. Everyone has suffered some very minor tumble, cut, or bruise, or hurt in childhood. Your suggestion here should be that you are now going back in time to the age of four or five, or perhaps six, to some time when you experienced a very minor hurt, nothing major. When hurt, a child naturally will cry and someone would probably comfort it, perhaps the mother. She would probably say, "Don't cry, don't cry, it's all right," or something similar. Repeat these phrases aloud several times, putting the expression into the words which would be used in comforting a child. If there is a feeling of other words being more appropriate, use them instead. If so, your subconscious is prompting the correct words that were actually said. The association of the sound of these words and their meaning helps to bring the regression.

Now look around in your mind's eye and form an impression of the scene. Are you indoors or outdoors? Try to bring it in clearer. Tell yourself it is now, just before you were slightly hurt, and note what you are doing. Then go to the moment of hurt and continue through what follows, hearing whatever was said. You probably will actually feel whatever hurt you, though not to the same degree.

When you have accomplished this, tell yourself you are now returning to the present time, in order to end the regression. (This should, of course, also follow your first regression attempt.) If you failed to remember this, no harm would be done, for you would soon reorient yourself to the present on awakening.

Most people can learn to regress in this way with no difficulty. If you cannot bring out an episode of a minor hurt, it may be that you unconsciously do not wish to remember any kind of unpleasant matter. You might then suggest return to some exceptionally pleasant or interesting experience at about the same age, one which may have been completely forgotten. Say to yourself, "I am now about five years old. Something very pleasant happened today. Perhaps it is Christmas or my birthday and I was given a nice present. Now I am back to it." You may then find yourself seeing a scene and reliving it. When it has fully developed, end it by the suggestion of returning to the present.

If you are not successful in producing these regressions, try again at another time. If you can go a bit deeper, without overdoing it, it would help. An important part of self-therapy consists of regressing to important past events which may be having a present effect.

In regressing as described here, you are reliving the experience as the participant. Sometimes if there is something unpleasant about the event, it is easier to see it as an observer, rather than taking part in it. When you find you are not entering the regression, try suggesting that you are going to see the scene and whatever happens as an observer, and that you will see yourself in the scene. This may overcome resistance to going back to something unpleasant, since being an observer is easier than taking part in the experience.

**An induction talk to aid in learning self-hypnosis.** If you have a tape recorder or a record player, the following induction talk can be recorded. This can be a great aid in learning self-hypnosis. Most larger record shops have facilities for cutting records, which is a simple, inexpensive matter. You could record your own voice or have someone else do this for you, either as a phonograph record or on tape.

In recording, a monotone voice is best and the words should be read quite slowly. The wording here includes induction and suggestions setting up a formula for you to follow for self-induction. When you have listened to your recording, or as soon as you have awakened at the end, you should put yourself back in hypnosis by following the formula as given.

Take any comfortable position in listening, either sitting in a comfortable chair or lying down. Let your arms rest on the arms of the chair, or lie beside you. Close your eyes and take two or three deep breaths. The talk follows:

Now that you are comfortable you will listen closely to my voice and will follow all the suggestions given. This will teach you how to enter hypnosis and how to produce it yourself. Your eyes are now closed. Take another deep breath, hold it a few seconds and let it out.

The more you can relax, the deeper you will be able to go into hypnosis. Let your muscles go as loose and limp as possible. To do this start with your right leg. Tighten the muscles first, making the leg rigid. Then let it relax from your toes up to your hip. Then tighten the muscles of the left leg. Let that leg relax from the toes up to the hip.

Let the stomach and abdominal area relax; then your chest and breathing muscles. The muscles of your back can loosen—your shoulders and neck muscles relaxing. Often we have tension in this area. Let all these muscles loosen. Now your arms from the shoulders right down to your finger tips. Even your facial muscles will relax. Relaxation is so pleasant and comfortable. Let go completely and enjoy the relaxation. All tension seems to drain away and you soon find a listlessness creeping over you, with a sense of comfort and well-being.

As you relax more and more, you will slip deeper and deeper into hypnosis. Your arms and legs may develop a feeling of heaviness. Or instead you may find your whole body feeling very light, as though you are floating on a soft cloud.

Now imagine that you are standing at the top of an escalator such as those in some stores. See the steps moving down in front of you, and see the railings. I am going to count from ten to zero. As I start to count, imagine you are stepping on the escalator, standing there with your hands on the railing while the steps move down in front of you taking you with them. If you prefer, you can imagine a staircase or an elevator instead. If you have any difficulty visualizing the escalator or staircase or elevator, just the count itself will take you deeper and deeper.

(Slowly) TEN—now you step on and start going down. NINE—EIGHT—SEVEN—SIX. Going deeper and deeper with each count. FIVE—FOUR—THREE. Still deeper. TWO—ONE —and ZERO. Now you step off at the bottom and will continue to go deeper still with each breath you take. Deeper and deeper with each breath. You are so relaxed and so comfortable. Let go still more. Notice your breathing. Probably it is now slower and you are breathing more from the bottom of your lungs, abdominal breathing.

In a moment you will notice that your hand and arm are beginning to lose any feeling of heaviness and are becoming light. If you are right-handed, it will be your right arm, if left-handed, it will be the left.

The arm is getting lighter and lighter. It will begin to lift. Perhaps just the fingers will move first, or the whole hand will start to float up. It will float up towards your face, as though your face was a magnet pulling it up until the fingers touch your face some place. Let's see where that will be. The arm begins to bend at the elbow. It is floating upward. If it has not started of its own accord, lift it voluntarily a few inches to give it a start. It will continue to go up of its own accord with no further effort. It floats on up toward your face, higher and higher.

The higher your hand goes the deeper you will go; the deeper you go, the higher the hand will go. Lifting, lifting, floating up higher and higher. Going higher and higher. Now if it has touched your face let your hand go down to any comfortable position. If it has not touched yet, it can continue to float up until it does touch. You can forget about the arm while I tell you how you can put yourself into hypnosis whenever you may wish to do so.

You will use much the same method being used now. When you have made yourself comfortable, you will merely close your eyes and drift into hypnosis. But in your first three or four practice sessions it would help you if you first lit a candle and when you have made yourself comfortable would look at the flickering flame for two or three minutes. Then close your eyes.

Then you will think to yourself the phrase, "Now I am going into hypnosis." Then repeat to yourself the words, "Relax now" three times, saying them very slowly. As you do this you will slip off into hypnosis. You say nothing aloud, you merely think these words. When you have done this, take another deep breath to help you relax more and go through the relaxation just as you have done before. Tell your muscles to relax as I have done.

When you have finally relaxed your arms, imagine the escalator, elevator or staircase. Now you should count backward from ten to zero, including the zero. Count slowly. In your first four practice sessions repeat the count three times, as though going down different levels. With practice you need only count once.

Whenever you are ready to awaken all you need to do is think to yourself, "Now I am going to wake up." Then count slowly to three and you will be wide awake. You will always awaken refreshed, relaxed and feeling fine.

While you are in hypnosis if something should happen so you should awaken, you will do so instantly and spontaneously—something such as the phone ringing or a real emergency like a fire. You will awaken instantly and be

wide awake and fully alert. Actually this would happen
without such a suggestion being necessary, for your subconscious mind always protects you.

Now I will count to three and you will be wide awake.
If convenient you should then go through this formula
for self-hypnosis and put yourself back in. You will re-
member the formula and go through it exactly as given.
Now awaken as I count. ONE. Coming awake now.
TWO—almost awake. THREE—now you are wide awake.
Wide awake.


## SUMMARY

You have now been introduced to several techniques in
self-hypnosis. Actually all hypnosis is really self-hypnosis.
The operator is only a guide and you do the work by
following his suggestions and accepting the ideas he
gives you. You now know how you can test your results
after you have practiced a bit, and you can learn from
your own subconscious the depth you have reached. You
know how you can regress to experiences which may
be affecting you in some way; through an understanding
of these, you should cease to be affected. You will be able
to use hypnosis not only in your program of self-betterment but in other ways as well.

In the next chapter you will learn how to use suggestion most effectively in your program.

# Chapter 5

# HOW THE USE OF
# AUTOSUGGESTION CAN
# IMPROVE YOUR LIFE

One of the best ways of influencing the subconscious mind is by means of suggestion. As has been mentioned, we all are suggestible in varying degrees, and extremely so while under hypnosis or the influence of a strong emotion. Sometimes suggestibility is mistakenly confused with gullibility, i.e., being easily fooled. If you were not suggestible you would find it difficult to learn. Being suggestible is an asset.

It is important to know the laws governing suggestion. Heterosuggestion (that given by someone else) is more potent than autosuggestion, but the latter can be quite effective, particularly with knowledge of how best to apply it. Even a light state of hypnosis increases suggestibility. Autohypnosis will shorten the time required in self-therapy and may uncover causes which can't otherwise be learned.

**How suggestion affects medical research.** The power of suggestion and the degree of suggestibility found in most people are continually seen when medical research is carried on to find out the effect of some new drug. In such research it is always necessary to use what is termed a "control" group of subjects. A number of people in one group are given the drug which is being tested. Another group is given a placebo

—something that looks like the real drug but is inert. Perhaps a sugar pill is used as the placebo.

The effect on both groups is studied. It will be found that a large percentage of the control group responds to the placebo just as do those who have taken the real drug. Suggestion causes this effect. In fact, the effect of suggestion is so great that it has been found necessary to keep those administering the drug in the dark as to which persons receive the drug and which ones get the placebo; otherwise, subjects manage to pick up clues from the person doing the testing.

**Rules to follow in making suggestions.** Suggestions may be permissive or commanding, direct or indirect, positive or negative. Autosuggestions will be direct rather than indirect. A positive one has much more force than a negative one. To make a suggestion positive, avoid such negative words as "not," "don't," "won't," and "can't." "I will not have a headache tomorrow" is a negative suggestion. "My head will be clear and I will feel well tomorrow" is positive.

A permissive suggestion is more likely to be carried out than a dominating command. Most of us resent being commanded to do something. The inner mind may resent it with autohypnosis and will be more cooperative as a rule if asked to do something rather than ordered to do it. But sometimes commands may be best. Individuals react differently. If there is an unconscious need to be dominated, then commands would be better. Phrasing a suggestion with the words "you can" is permissive; "you will" is a command.

Repetition is the main rule in making suggestions work. They should be repeated three or four times, or even more. All advertising is based on suggestion and advertisers know that the effect of repeated ads is cumulative. Commercials on TV are repeated again and again, as you have undoubtedly noted to your annoyance. (As a side observation, because of this annoyance, results from TV commercials would be far greater if advertisers knew more of the principles and laws of suggestion and of psychology. When annoyed, many people make it a point not to buy a product so advertised.)

Time must be allowed for a suggestion to be accepted by the subconscious and then carried out. It should be put in the immediate future, rather than the immediate present. To say "My headache is gone" is contrary to fact as it could not disappear instantly. "My head will begin to clear; soon the ache will dwindle away and I will feel fine" allows time for the idea to be carried out.

Autosuggestions may be made verbally, though it usually is not necessary to say the words aloud. Thinking them is enough. However, you should experiment as to this since some of us do respond better if they are said aloud.

If a visual image can be formed and added to a verbal suggestion, it will make the suggestion more potent. There is a tendency on the part of the subconscious to carry out any prolonged and repeated visual image. It will depend on the type of suggestion you use whether or not a visual image can be added.

An example of a visual image: you are tired at the end of the day and wish to overcome this by suggestion. After suggesting that you will begin to feel refreshed, visualize yourself doing something where you are full of "vim, vigor and vitality." In your mind's eye see yourself playing golf or tennis or some other sport, or merely walking briskly around the block swinging your arms, chest out and obviously full of pep. Carry this thought for three or four minutes. The results of such suggestions can be quite surprising in overcoming fatigue. The visual image should always represent the result desired.

Another example: in treating an obese woman, I instructed her to obtain a photograph of herself when she was slender. She did not have one, so I told her to cut a picture from a magazine of a girl in a bathing suit, and take the head from some picture of herself and paste it on this magazine picture. She was then to place this picture on her mirror and to look at it every time she looked in the mirror, thinking "That is I." When she went to bed at night, she was directed to visualize herself as she would like to be, like the body in the picture.

Establishing a motive for acceptance of a suggestion is helpful. Arousing some emotion and "hooking" it to a suggestion will make it more effective. This may be by means of words or a visual image or both. Desire for success can be the emotion aroused.

In giving yourself a suggestion, acceptance by the inner mind is needed or it will not be carried out, no matter how much you may consciously want this. When a permissive suggestion has been repeated and no result shown, it would be well to try a command instead of being permissive.

You can learn through ideomotor replies to questions

whether or not your subconscious has accepted a suggestion. If not, perhaps further questioning can locate the reason why it has been rejected. If a pendulum or finger answer promises acceptance, it is almost certain to be carried out.

**Some further rules about suggestion.** The subconscious should not be burdened with too many suggestions at one time. It is better to work on only one thing at a time, or at most two. The effect becomes diffused otherwise. Work with repetition on one or two suggestions for two or three sessions. If other ends are sought, use suggestion on another one or two for a few times, then go back and repeat the first ones.

Word your suggestions with only the end result in mind. Be specific as to your goal. Your inner mind knows far better than your conscious mind how to reach the goal. Stimulate it into action and it will find the best means.

Some writers have made quite a point as to the wording of suggestions—whether the personal pronoun should be *I* or *you*, first person or second. Perhaps you should experiment as to this but I believe the subconscious takes either as applying to you. I think this is proved by the fact that, in therapy, suggestions which have been picked up as fixed ideas, and are then carried out, are found to be worded either way or both. This kind of suggestion will be considered in a later chapter.

Suggestibility can work both ways. Negative suggestions can also be effective. We are constantly bombarded with suggestions. An unpleasant trick can be played on an individual in an office. When he arrives in the morning a fellow worker greets him with the remark, "Good heavens, Jim, you must have had a bad night. You really look terrible this morning." Jim has been feeling quite well and is surprised at this statement. A few minutes later someone remarks casually, "Got a hangover this morning, Jim? You sure look bad." Another inquires sympathetically if he perhaps has a fever. By this time Jim is feeling poorly and any further repetition is likely to send him home actually ill.

One important part of self-therapy is to locate and dehypnotize yourself of negative and detrimental suggestions which may be affecting you. We all carry these suggestions with us; for the most part we are unaware of them.

In his book, *Self-Suggestion* (Huna Research Publications, Vista, California), Max Long advocates the use of

deep breathing while giving oneself suggestions. Long
recommends breathing deeply and hard, at the same time
concentrating intently on the suggestion and "pulsing"
the thoughts. By this he means to concentrate for a moment, then pause, and start concentrating again, continuing to repeat this, all the while breathing deeply.
Long adds that belief and firm conviction bring the best
results.

Dr. James Hixson, a Hollywood dentist who is one of
the instructors with Hypnosis Symposiums, recommends
a short cut in giving autosuggestions. He advises writing
out in detail exactly what you wish to accomplish. Then
condense the idea into a sentence or two, omitting details
but stating the results desired. From these sentences select
a key word or very brief phrase which includes the entire
suggestion you have first written out. This key word or
phrase is to be repeated several times to yourself, after
which your thoughts should be diverted to something entirely different.

**Emil Coué and his ideas.** During the nineteen twenties
there was quite a vogue in the use of autosuggestion for
self-benefit, though it was much greater in Europe than
in this country. Coué, Baudouin, Pierce, and others, all
wrote books on the subject. I would recommend Pierce's
*Mobilizing the Mid-Brain* (Putnam & Sons, New York
—out of print but obtainable sometimes in used book-
stores) as being the best, though Baudouin's also is very
good. Coué operated a clinic on autosuggestion in Nancy,
France, and became world famous from his successes. He
was really a pharmacist but made quite a study of the
psychology of suggestion. Europeans used his principles
and found them of great value. When Coué made a lecture tour in the United States, skeptical newspapermen
ridiculed him and scoffed at his ideas so that his tour
was a failure.

Coué did not deserve this ridicule heaped upon him,
for his ideas are sound. One of his techniques was to repeat again and again each day the suggestion "Every day,
in every way, I am getting better and better." In his
earlier work with suggestion he made use of specific, detailed verbalizations. Often these were successful. But
later he decided that the general, nonspecific suggestion,
deliberately avoiding telling the subconscious how to
achieve an end, was better. Such a suggestion would include all that one might be aiming at, not one particular
goal. The formula has definite merit. Although Coué's

methods were never accepted to any extent in this country, he had quite a following in Europe, and many benefited from his work.

Coué was the first to make an exhaustive study of suggestion and its effects. He formulated several important ideas and laws about suggestion. One he termed the law of reversed effect. Coué said, "If one thinks, 'I should like to do this but I can't' (a negative thought), the harder he tries, the less he is able." Somewhat along the same line is the effect of using the word *try* about something. Saying "I'll try" implies doubt—the expectation of failure. An attempt at something should be approached positively; you are going to do it, not try to do it!

An example of the law of reversed effect is seen in the following situation. If a 12-foot board, a foot wide, is laid on the ground, one can walk it hardly giving it a glance. Place it between two chairs three feet above the ground and there would still be no difficulty in walking its length. A little more care would be used. Place it between two buildings ten stories in the air and try to walk it! Fear and doubt would enter and the law of reversed effect would take hold. The walker would probably fall off, or not be able to venture out on the board at all.

Another common example of the working of this law is seen in the person troubled with insomnia. He goes to bed with the thought (a negative suggestion) "I suppose I'll not be able to go to sleep." Then he tries and the harder he tries to go to sleep, the wider awake he becomes. When he stops trying, sometime later, thoroughly fatigued, and begins to think of something else, he drops off to sleep within a few minutes.

Baudouin cites another illustration of this law. A person learning to ride a bicycle, still unsure of his balance, sees a tree ahead of him. His doubts arise and he is sure to run into the tree while trying desperately to avoid it.

Coué made a sage observation—"When the imagination and the will are in conflict, the imagination always wins." In effect this is saying that the subconscious will always win over the conscious mind when they conflict. It certainly is true.

Still another of Coué's contributions was what he called the law of dominant effort—an idea always tends towards realization and a stronger emotion always counteracts a weaker one.

## SUMMARY

In this chapter you have learned something of the power of suggestion. You will find it of great value in your self-betterment program. Keep your suggestions permissive for the most part, though sometimes you may need to prod your subconscious in a more commanding way. Remember the need to repeat, to stress motivations for acceptance, not to give too many suggestions at one time, to use visual imagery where it is possible, and to suggest results, not means.

You would find Coué's formula of "every day, in every way, I'm getting better and better" helpful if you will repeat it to yourself on rising in the morning and on going to bed at night, which is what he recommended. It will only take a moment or two of your time.

*Chapter 6*

# ELIMINATE EMOTIONAL
# TROUBLES FROM YOUR LIFE

In order to deal with whatever emotional problems or illnesses you may have, you should know how they originate—the factors causing them. Then you will better be able to change or eliminate them.

**Some Freudian ideas.** Aside from hereditary factors, we are the product of our environment and of the things which happen to us as we grow up and live our lives. Undoubtedly the first few years of childhood are of the utmost importance in this process of conditioning and maturing. Freud placed most of the responsibility for emotional difficulties on these childhood experiences and the conflicts which develop from them. Freudian psychoanalysis aims largely at bringing into conscious awareness a realization of how these things affect us. Other psychotherapists assign less importance to childhood; with them, the important problems are those that relate to the present rather than the past.

The usual psychiatric treatment of mental problems and conditions to a large extent follows Freud, though of necessity it is often modified considerably. Such usual treatment is likely to be a long, drawn-out matter and therefore very expensive. Most psychoanalysts follow Freudian methods rigidly. Psychoanalysis has become a cult with a definite ritual. For example, Freud in his younger days was quite a shy person and felt uncomfortable when a patient sat facing him and watching him.

Therefore he had his patients lie on a couch while he sat at its head where he could not be seen. Analysts ritualistically follow this same procedure today. It must be the best way because Freud used it!

As a rule psychoanalysis requires anywhere from 300 to 600 hours. A patient is customarily seen for an hour a day, five days a week. The method is essentially passive, the analyst making some interpretations and comments, and at times giving some direction to the therapy but usually letting the patient talk of whatever comes to mind —free association.

In some deep-seated neuroses and other conditions, long-term therapy is a necessity. It would be difficult to overcome these conditions otherwise and self-therapy would be of little help. Of course this means much expense. A complete psychoanalysis is only for the wealthy, with fees amounting to thousands of dollars. Most emotional conditions, other than insanity, can be briefly, and perhaps even more successfully, treated with other methods.

**Pavlov and conditioned reflexes.** Pavlovian theories are based on the idea of conditioned reflexes. In the early years of this century the Russian physiologist Ivan Pavlov conducted his famous experiments with dogs, showing how conditioned reflexes develop. The dogs were fed when hungry and at the same time a bell was rung. When this was repeated a number of times, the dog would salivate whenever the bell was rung, although food was not given at the same time. It had learned to associate the sound of the bell with food. The bell then stimulated a flow of saliva. Salivation was the conditioned reflex which had been established.

Humans are just as subject to the development of conditioned reflexes as are dogs. We respond to some stimulus, a word, or situation which seems to have no bearing or relationship to the responsive behavior, yet the stimulus is associated in some such way, as was the bell with food. We may be unaware that we are responding to such a stimulus; it will often trigger off behavior or thoughts which then may seem quite senseless. We probably will try to rationalize why we have acted in this peculiar way.

Most conditioning is of definite value to us. Conditioned responses become automatic and we do not have to think how to carry them out. Habits and skills often develop from such reflexes. However, conditioning may work in the wrong direction and be detrimental. Responses may stir up feelings of guilt, hostility, anger and other emotions which may be harmful because of the way we react to them. Neurotic patterns are largely derived from conditioning.

Psychiatry in other than the English-speaking countries is aimed largely at the removal of conditioned reflexes which are found to be causing emotional difficulties. Often words are the trigger mechanism or stimulus setting off the reflex, and general semantics is thus involved. The Russian psychiatrist Platinov in a book entitled *The Word* (published in Russia and printed in English), says that many Russian psychiatrists use hypnosis to uncover the conditioned reflexes and their stimuli. The patient is then caused to go back in memory to the time or event when a reflex was established. Understanding the association tends to wipe out the response. This is really a dehypnotizing of the patient. Conditioned reflexes are almost identical at times with post-hypnotic suggestions. Platinov claims successful results with 78 per cent of his cases. If true, this a far better record than Freudian methods can show.

Dr. Joseph Wolpe, a South African psychiatrist now in the United States, has written of his development of a method of psychotherapy (*Psychotherapy Through Reciprocal Inhibition*, Stanford University Press, Stanford, California) very similar to the Russian approach. He also uses hypnosis to recondition his patients and claims the same degree of success. Some of his techniques lend themselves readily to self-help and will be described.

**How suggestion is used in therapy.** Another type of psychotherapy involves the use of suggestions. They may be directed at the subconscious mind by the person himself (autosuggestion) or may be given by some one else (heterosuggestion). Probably the latter is somewhat more effective but self-suggestion also can be very valuable. It is most successful when hypnosis is utilized.

Prior to the acceptance of Freudian ideas about a half century ago, suggestion was the only known method of psychotherapy. During the period roughly from 1880 to about 1900 or a little later this type of hypnotic treatment through suggestion was used extensively and with good results. One of the foremost physicians of his time in France was Hyppolite Bernheim. He learned about hypnosis and suggestion from a modest country doctor named Lieubeault who practiced in Nancy. Bernheim joined Lieubeault in his practice and they conducted a clinic together. In the course of some twenty years they treated over 30,000 patients with suggestion under hypnosis. Their success was such that many physicians from all over Europe went to Nancy to study under them. Freud was one of them.

Freud then attempted to use hypnosis in his early experimental work. This was in association with another psychiatrist named Breuer. Breuer was one of the leading medical hypnotists of his day, while Freud was a young beginner. Freud was under the impression that a deep state of hypnosis was necessary for treatment, but he found only a small percentage of people could be deeply hypnotized. He really knew little about hypnosis and was a very poor hypnotist. He lacked confidence in himself at that time and for good results in the induction of hypnosis confidence is very important.

Freud could not tolerate his failures, when Breuer was so successful. He therefore sought other methods and techniques, arriving at free association and dream interpretation. He then gave up the use of hypnosis. Because of this, his followers, including most psychiatrists, have believed hypnosis to be worthless in psychotherapy. Most psychiatrists are completely uninformed about it and do not know its modern applications. Many still think it is applied only as a matter of suggestion as Bernheim used it.

A Freudian idea accepted by most psychiatrists is that treatment by suggestion is dangerous in that if a symptom is removed by suggestion, a worse one will form. The use of hypnosis has been attacked on this basis by some psychiatrists writing in popular magazines and also in medical journals. Many who have read such articles are therefore fearful of hypnosis.

The idea involved is that behind any symptom is an energy seeking an outlet. The symptom is the outlet. If the symptom is removed by suggestion, the energy is then blocked and will seek a new outlet. For example, if an alcoholic were to be given suggestions removing the desire to drink, or preventing drinking, he might then turn to narcotics instead.

This idea of some energy being present seems farfetched. No such energy can be measured or demonstrated in any way. Certainly there may be an unconscious need for a symptom. It may serve a purpose. Quite overlooked by such critics is the fact that no amount of suggestion would cause elimination of a symptom if the need for it is very strong. Hypnotic suggestions are only effective if acceptable to the subject, acceptable both consciously and subconsciously. Every experienced hypnotherapist knows this. A symptom may be removed by hypnotic suggestion, but many times this fails and the symptom persists. Also, experienced hypnotherapists know that suggestions to eliminate a symptom should always be given on a permissive basis rather than as hypnotic commands. This is a safeguard which completely obviates any possible danger in symptom removal, even if the Freudian concept of some mysterious energy were correct.

Dr. Roy Dorcus, a prominent psychologist, recently presented a paper at a meeting on hypnosis at the University of Kansas. He pointed out that most medical treatment, other than the use of antibiotics or the sulfa drugs in infectious diseases, is nothing but symptom removal. Treatment with other drugs usually is only aimed at a symptom, not its cause. Aspirin for a headache merely removes the symptom. Critics of symptom removal by suggestion routinely treat their own patients with the tranquilizer drugs to overcome depression. This is symptom removal. Drugs are regarded as safe and proper for symptom removal; if done by suggestion it is dangerous. Of course this is quite ridiculous. The supposed energy would also seek another outlet following removal of a symptom by drugs.

In the cases cited by psychiatrists where other symptoms have supposedly formed, or where some other bad effect has followed use of hypnosis, the conclusion was made that the result came from ending the symptom. As a matter of fact it may have been from some entirely different cause. Some other need, entirely unrelated to the original symptom, may have stimulated the other symptom or the bad result which later developed.

## THE SEVEN MOST COMMON FACTORS
## CAUSING EMOTIONAL TROUBLES
## AND ILLNESSES

The causes of harmful behavior patterns, of emotional illness, and of wrong thinking and unfavorable character traits are found to vary considerably. Methods of self-therapy, therefore, must also be variable. However, these methods will apply in self-help no matter what the objective.

**Conflict.** One of the most common causes of emotional difficulty is conflict. Freud believed conflict to be the common denominator in emotional difficulties of most types. Conflict arises when we have a need or wish to do something, but the taboos of society or conscience prevent. Sex, of course, is probably the greatest source of conflict.

Frequently we repress our conflicts, thrusting them out of consciousness because they are too unpleasant, or because we feel guilty about them. Aggressiveness and hostility are emotions likely to be repressed. Memories of unpleasant or frightening experiences may be so treated. They remain in the subconscious, however, and may then cause continual trouble. Then we may consciously be unaware of why some difficulty has resulted.

In self-therapy it is possible to remove these repressions and bring back memories to awareness. Sometimes the repression may be too strong and help from a psychotherapist is needed. Of course many conflicts are not suppressed and we know about them consciously. Ordinarily these are not difficult to resolve with self-therapy. Case histories will be given to show the results of conflict and of the various other likely causative factors which are noted here.

Aside from conflicts, other causes which may enter are: (1) motivation, (2) the effect of suggestion, (3) organ language, (4) identification, (5) masochism or self-punishment, and (6) past experiences, especially traumatic ones. In some conditions perhaps only one of these seven possible causative factors may enter, but it is more usual for more than one to be present. Sometimes, though rarely, all might be found.

**Motivations.** Locating the motives for a symptom or condition or behavior pattern involves learning what purpose it may serve. An illness may bring sympathy and attention for which there may be a strong neurotic need. A child whose parents neglect him may find that illness brings attention, and it also may serve to keep him out of school which he dislikes.

Barbara F., 21 years old, had been married for about a year to a very brilliant and good-looking young man. He was a college graduate and she had only finished high school. Shy, with strong feelings of inferiority and insecurity, she suffered from a headache which had been

continuous for more than four months. It was not so
severe as to incapacitate her, but bothered her all day
long. Sometimes drugs could modify it, but it persisted.
Her family physician was unable to find any organic
reason for the headache, despite many tests, including
neurological ones. Therefore he believed the condition
probably had some emotional basis.

It was not difficult to bring out that Barbara was using
the headaches to bring sympathy and attention from her
parents and also from her husband, to whom she felt inferior. It was pointed out to her that she might better
interest herself more in her husband's activities and could
read and study to bring her education nearer his level. It
was obvious that he was much in love with her. When she
realized that her behavior was very immature, the headache quickly disappeared.

A common motive for a symptom is that of defense.
Barbara really was defending herself with her headache. It
must be learned just what the symptom protects against.
It may well be an attempt to escape from problems and
reality. In migraine headache there usually are strong
feelings of hostility, aggression, and frustration present.
Such emotions are suppressed as objectionable. The headaches seem to result from bottling up these emotions and
may also function as self-punishment from guilt over
having such feelings. These same factors are sometimes
present in bursitis and arthritic conditions, and in still
others. Such symptoms may serve to protect against aggressive actions which might be taken because of emotions of hostility and anger.

Another case, with an entirely different type of motivation, was that of a businessman, Mr. G., who had lost his
voice. This condition is called aphonia. He could speak
in only a low, hoarse whisper. His physician could find
no reason for this as his vocal cords were normal. When
placed in hypnosis Mr. G. was able to speak with no
difficulty, which proved conclusively that the condition
was emotional. He soon was able to bring out the reasons
for his trouble. His business was in excellent condition;
he was expanding it rapidly and his sales had almost
doubled over the previous year's sales. However he was
very short of capital, had borrowed heavily, was buying
supplies to fill his orders, and could not meet his bills.
Within a few months money would be coming in to take
care of this, but his creditors were plaguing him with de-
mands for payment and with threats. Most were local

firms and his phone was busy with calls asking for payment. By losing his voice he was still able to give orders in his plant, but he could not talk over the phone. The condition was an effort to escape from unpleasant explaining.

It was suggested that Mr. G. write a letter to each creditor enclosing a financial statement and information on his excellent sales, with promise to pay within three or four months. This would undoubtedly satisfy his creditors. When he had done this, he quickly recovered his voice.

One type of neurosis is technically labeled *hysteria.* This should not be confused with the term hysterics, which is an emotional reaction rather than an emotional illness. With hysteria a symptom might develop such as paralysis of a limb, or functional blindness. Such a symptom of course is not organic. The motive for the paralysis might be a means of escaping from something, or perhaps it could be to prevent the person from attacking someone.

Functional blindness could be a result of seeing something about which the person felt very guilty, or it could serve to prevent the person from seeing something unpleasant which he wishes to avoid seeing. And of course there could be many other motives. This type of condition has been called a *conversion* symptom. Less disabling ones are very common.

**Effects of suggestion.** Everyone is suggestible to some extent or we would not be able to learn. Suggestibility should not be confused with gullibility. One of the most effective ways of making suggestions effective is repetition, impressing them on the subconscious. As children we may repeatedly be told something until it is unconsciously accepted and then carried out. If a child is not doing well in school and is reproached again and again by a parent with such remarks as "You are just stupid; you can't seem to learn," such statements may be accepted and believed by the child. He may then become unable to learn easily, although of good intelligence.

Many psychotherapists unfamiliar with hypnosis fail to realize the power and the effects of suggestion. It is one of the most common causes of emotional difficulties. Failure to locate and remove such suggestions will prevent successful treatment. A definite part of therapy is to "dehypnotize" the individual and remove such suggestions.

A trait or symptom may be largely or entirely caused by some statement which becomes a fixed idea in the subconscious mind. It is a conditioned reflex and is carried out exactly as if it were a posthypnotic suggestion. When we are under the influence of an emotion we seem to become more suggestible, just as when in hypnosis, and a fixed idea of this type is often set up at such a time, or it may result from being repeated again and again. A posthypnotic suggestion is one given when a person is in hypnosis but which is executed later after he has been awakened.

Dr. George Estabrooks of Colgate University has written (*Hypnotism*, Dutton, New York) that under an emotion the subconscious mind seems to register a statement just as if a phonograph record was being made. When some association restimulates it, the idea involved will then be carried out compulsively, as would a posthypnotic suggestion.

To give an example of this, while I was giving a course in Mexico City to a group of physicians, teaching them to use hypnosis, a demonstration in treating a patient was made. One member of the class, Dr. R., was a woman about forty years old who said she had suffered from chronic diarrhea all her life. Medical treatment had never helped. Under hypnosis it was brought out that the main cause of her condition resulted from an experience at eighteen months of age. She had then had a digestive illness so severe that her parents expected her to die and had even bought a cemetery lot for her burial.

Instructed to recall this incident completely, Dr. R. told of being held in her mother's arms, feeling very ill. Her parents were crying and the doctor was saying to them, "She will never get over this." The statement was made in Spanish. With finger movements in response to questions, she was asked if this remark by the physician was the reason she had retained the symptom of diarrhea. To the child it had been the main part of her illness. The answer was affirmative. The next question was, "Now that you realize this and know you did not die and did recover from the illness except for this symptom, can you now be free of it?" The finger response was again affirmative. When seen again about six months later, Dr. R. told me she had had no more diarrhea following this single session.

A question here would be as to how a child of only 18 months of age would understand language, in this case the remark of the physician. A possible e               d be that the subconscious at an early age may register

speech merely as sounds. After language is learned it can then understand the meaning and would carry out the idea or suggestion involved. A person under hypnosis going back and "replaying" a past experience will say he hears what people are saying. This might be imagination or fantasy and it would be difficult to prove that such words were actually said. In the case of the woman physician, and in many other cases, it would seem highly probable that there is a definite memory of what was said, since the removal of the suggestion brought loss of the symptom.

This same phrase, "She'll never get over it," was involved in another case where a middle-aged woman suffered from a chronic cough. She told me this had persisted for as long as she could remember and she had long ago stopped trying to treat it. Now she wondered if it could be stopped through hypnosis. With questioning she learned that the symptom began when she was four years old and had had a serious illness with whooping cough and complications. Again the doctor had told her parents that she would never get over it, meaning that she would die. She recovered but had heard what the doctor said and kept the coughing symptom.

A rather funny effect of suggestion was brought out by an attractive young woman. While working with her, she was regressed to a time when she was ten years old when her mother was punishing her. While beating her with a switch the mother cried, "Don't you ever say no again! Don't ever say that word no again!"

As she told what was happening the young woman sat up and remarked, "You know, I've been so ashamed sometimes. I've never been able to say no. And some of the things I've done because I just couldn't say no!"

Most surgeons and anesthetists are quite unaware that the subconscious part of the mind hears at all times, during sleep, while you are unconscious from a blow, or when under drug anesthesia. Dr. David Cheek has written in medical journals about this, as has Dr. L. S. Wolfe, an anesthesiologist. It can easily be demonstrated with hypnosis by regressing a subject to the time of an operation. What was said or done during the operation can then be brought out, something which is very surprising to physicians.

In this way, adverse suggestions can be picked up by the subconscious. Wolfe believes that some deaths on the operating table have resulted from some remark, for instance, the surgeon saying "It's malignant. The patient hasn't a chance."

On the other hand surgeons and anesthesiologists familiar with this truth make it a point to reassure the patient undergoing surgery and to give suggestions for quick healing, for freedom from postoperative nausea, and to prevent shock.

Richard S. was a young man of thirty. He had had more than a year of psychoanalysis but results were not satisfactory and he had visited me in the hopes that hypnosis could help him with some of his problems. During one of his visits he told of having a strong hatred for his father.

"I can't understand why I feel this way about him," said Richard. "He's a physician and he has always treated me well. He never was strict or punished me unless I needed it. I have a lot of admiration for him, but I really hate him. It has given me quite a conflict."

After questioning, which located an experience which seemed to be the cause of this hatred, Richard was hypnotized and told to regress to the incident. He was 18 years old and was undergoing an operation to remove his tonsils. He had been given ether as an anesthetic and was "out" on the operating table. He told of his father entering the room.

"That's funny," he said. "I never knew my father was there but I hear him. And he is saying something about me. He calls me a little bastard. That's why I hate him. I've often wondered if he really is my father and if I might be a bastard."

He was asked to repeat what his father said.

"He says, 'Why you little bastard. You're just a bastard.' But he's not saying it to me. He says it to the surgeon, Dr. Jamison. Dr. Jamison tells him he can't stay—he tells him to get out and father is angry and says this to him. They are friends, though."

"Now that you realize your father did not call you a bastard can you realize that you don't need to hate him any more and can have a good feeling for him?"

"Sure I can. That explains it. He didn't mean me. What a relief to know what caused it!"

Richard's father was visiting him at the time and was asked if he remembered being in the operating room when his son underwent his tonsillectomy. He confirmed everything Richard had said, told of his anger at being ejected by his colleague. He had realized his son's attitude towards him and had been hurt and puzzled by it. Their relation-ship became very close afterwards.

**Organ language.** In psychology this is a most interesting matter. There are many phrases which we commonly use in speaking about something unpleasant. The subconscious may translate the idea expressed in such a phrase into an actual physical condition. Examples of these phrases are: *It's a pain in the neck; it makes me sick; I can't swallow that; that gives me a pain; it makes me sick at my stom-ach; that's a headache to me; it makes me tired.* There are lots of others. When we use such phrases the actual condition we mention may develop.

Mr. H., a businessman, was sent to me because he had a bad taste in his mouth for which his physician could find no reason. Because everything tasted so bad, he ate very little and had lost much weight.

During one of his visits he told of having been called as a witness in a trial. Then man on trial was the head of a large company with which Mr. H. did business. In fact the greatest part of his sales were to this man. Mr. H. was afraid he would be asked a certain question which, if he answered truthfully, would cause his customer to be convicted. Mr. H. would then lose his business as a result, which would be a calamity for him. Fortunately the question was not asked at the trial.

In telling about it he remarked, "That trial certainly left a bad taste in my mouth!" He immediately realized what he had said and inquired, "Do you suppose that's why I've had this bad taste? It started right after that trial." Of course this was correct. Involved also were guilt feelings because he knew his customer had done some-thing criminal which had cost his company a loss of several hundred thousand dollars. Mr. H. felt he should have informed the district attorney of what he knew, as a civic duty. He had selfishly condoned a criminal act for his own benefit.

It was pointed out to him how he was endangering his health and thus was affecting his innocent family in so punishing himself. He was asked if perhaps his duty to his own family was not of greater importance than his civic duty. With this argument and an understanding of the mechanism behind his symptom, it quickly dis-appeared.

**Identification.** All children are imitative, as any parent knows. Children frequently try to be like their parents and sometimes will copy the behavior of others also who are close to them. This stems normally from love for a parent. Even a hated parent may be imitated because he seems all-powerful; he tells the child what he can or cannot do, and he punishes the child. The young one wants to be big and strong and powerful like the hated parent. Sometimes, also, imitation results from being told again and again such statements "You are just like your father."

This form of behavior is called *identification*. Identification means dramatization. The attempt to be like a parent will produce similar traits, even some illness which the parent may have. If a mother is greatly overweight, her child may identify with her and become overweight. This is a frequent factor in obesity. Often it is difficult to know whether something is inherited or if it is merely identification. Undoubtedly everyone identifies in this way at times and these childhood identifications are carried into adult life as habits.

A dentist once visited me bothered with an itching ear. He said he had been to dermatologists and ear specialists who were unable to find any physical involvement. He wondered if it might be psychological. During treatment he was asked if anyone close to him had had such a condition.

"Oh, yes," he replied, "My mother's ear itched in just the same way and she was always scratching it with her little finger, just as I do. And as she got older she got a bit deaf in that ear. I don't think I hear quite as well now, either."

He had been extremely fond of his mother and quite dependent on her, as he related. Identification was explained to him and finger responses to questions confirmed that this was the reason for his itching ear.

**Masochism.** None of us wear wings and it is only human nature at times to do things that we regret and to have the wrong kind of thoughts. The subconscious mind may then decide that such thoughts or actions require punishment. It would even seem that the nicest people are most likely to have strong guilt feelings and then to punish themselves. They have an overgrown conscience and punishment may be over very minor matters.

The worst criminals are often psychopaths who apparently lack a conscience, although some criminals do feel very guilty. Undoubtedly many who commit crimes are apprehended because of an unconscious need to be caught and punished. They do something leading to capture or betrayal of themselves.

Most of us show masochism at times. The neurotic person may exaggerate this to a great extent, sometimes to a point of self-destruction. Dr. Karl Menninger, a prominent psychiatrist, has discussed this in his book *Man Against Himself* (Harcourt Brace, New York). Extreme self-punishment may bring actual suicide or a fatal psychosomatic illness.

Masochism is a frequent part of emotionally caused disease and to overcome it the sources of guilt should be explored. The goal then is acceptance by the subconscious that punishment is no longer necessary. A common factor in alcoholism is unconscious self-destruction.

The need to be hurt sometimes may lead a person to become accident or operation prone. The wise physician will suspect masochism in a patient when he finds in taking a case history that the person has had many different operations. In psychosomatic illness it is a possible factor whenever the condition is a painful one.

Dentists frequently have patients come to them needing a tooth extraction, having previously lost a number of teeth. With many perfectly good teeth remaining, the patient may demand extraction of the rest, claiming he no longer wants to be bothered with them. This, of course, is a rationalization. What he really wants is to be hurt. His case history is sure to show many past operations performed on him.

One of my patients was a very nice woman in her thirties whom we will call Helen. Of course names given here are not real names to protect patients from identification. Helen was the worst masochist I have ever encountered. She was a beauty but had married a worthless husband, unconsciously believing she did not deserve a better man. She always had cuts or bruises on her body and frequently was ill with one ailment or another. She would fall down and hurt herself, run into doors, and damage herself in other ways.

Helen told of her childhood, saying that as far back as she could remember her mother had beat her every day of her life. Of course the mother was a sadist, for the daughter was so terrified of her that she was always obedient and good. When Helen was 16 and too big for such punishment, her mother adopted other ways to hurt her.

As a result of all this, the girl unconsciously had decided that she must be a horrible, wicked creature to warrant such treatment from her mother. Acceptance of this image of herself led her to punish herself when she grew older and no longer lived at home. The girl's subconscious then took over the job of punishment.

**Past experiences.** Many of the situations mentioned here originate in past experiences. Past events of one kind or another are usually implicated in psychosomatic illness and other disturbances. Guilt feelings arise from past happenings, as do suggestions. Unacceptable ideas and thoughts originate in the past. Uncovering these episodes is an important part of psychotherapy.

Another important type of occurrence is the traumatic one, where a person has had a bad fright or shock. The death of a loved one is a great trauma. Such incidents, being so unpleasant, frequently are repressed. Recalling them, with accompanying understanding, helps to rid oneself of their effects.

One of the possible causes of stuttering is sometimes a trauma, though there probably would be other causes as well. John D. was in his mid-twenties and had stuttered badly since he was three years old. Under hypnosis, by means of finger responses, it was learned that he had suffered a very frightening occurrence when three years old. Until then he had spoken normally for his age.

John had been very fond of a little dog which belonged to next door neighbors, and often played with the animal. One day the neighbor's home caught fire. Fire equipment arrived with sirens blaring. Other neighbors came out to watch and there was much excitement. John's mother carried him out to see. The house next door was now blazing furiously. As they looked, the little dog sprang onto a window seat where they could see him. A blazing curtain fell on him and his fur took fire. As they watched, he burned and died. John shrieked in terror and went into convulsions from shock. From then on he had stuttered. When the emotions from this trauma had been worked off, his speech rapidly improved and in a few weeks he talked in a normal way.

Strangely, most stutterers are excellent hypnotic subjects and when in hypnosis most find that they can talk perfectly well. When awakened, they again stutter.

In self-treatment, all of these seven points as described here should be explored. By ideomotor answers to ques-

tions, it will be learned which ones are involved and which
ones can be eliminated as having no bearing. These are
the seven keys with which you can open the doors to
health and happiness.

## SUMMARY

In this chapter you have read of the ideas which both
Freud and Pavlov developed as to the origin of emotional illnesses and other psychological difficulties. Their
theories are both correct and properly should be considered in combination when treating these conditions.

You have learned how suggestion is used in therapy
and that it is not dangerous to remove a symptom by
suggestion.

The seven keys to be used in ridding yourself of such
conditions should be reviewed. They are the underlying
causes which can be located and brought to light by
ideomotor questioning. Digestion of the insight you get
into these causes should cause them to disappear. One
or more, even all seven, may be involved.

They are: conflicts, motivation, the effect of suggestion, organ language, identification, self-punishment, and
the effect of past experiences. In your self-treatment program you will look for these in yourself.

# Chapter 7

# HOW BAD EMOTIONS
# INJURE YOUR HEALTH

When we suffer from emotional troubles their results take widely different forms. Why some particular form occurs is not always easy to understand. Most, if not all of us, have developed some character traits and habits of thinking which are harmful at times, perhaps greatly so. They can be tremendous handicaps. No one likes to think of himself as neurotic, but we all can develop neurotic symptoms of one type or another. It is a part of being human. It would be impossible for anyone to be so well-adjusted and so free from psychological disturbances as never to have had a psychosomatic illness. Even a cold may have emotional causes. Many accidents are unconsciously self-inflicted. Even a slip of the tongue is subconsciously motivated.

The most severe mental illnesses are the psychoses. However, a neurosis may also be a severe condition, completely incapacitating a person. In this book we are not concerned with psychotic states and severe neuroses, for these require treatment by a psychotherapist and little could be accomplished with self-treatment.

**When self-therapy is not advisable.** There are some contraindications to self-therapy, although most people can safely undertake this and can expect good results. A psychotic certainly should be in the hands of a psychiatrist and probably should be in an institution, this depending somewhat on the form and severity of the

86

condition. He may be unaware of his condition and thus it is unlikely that he will treat himself in any way. Quite a few people believe they are on the verge of insanity when very disturbed, but may be far from it. If one is extremely disturbed, this is one reason to avoid self-treatment.

A neurosis bad enough to make the person incapacitated would hardly be helped by self-therapy. The degree would be important here. A nervous breakdown is a form of neurosis and treatment by a therapist is essential. If you suffer from strong anxiety, are often extremely depressed with possible thoughts of suicide, you should have treatment but not by yourself. More extreme sexual aberrations, such as homosexuality, would have small benefit without the guidance of a psychotherapist.

The forms taken by an actual neurosis are usually classified as anxiety states, probably the most common neurosis, phobias, obsessions, compulsions, hysteria and extreme character disorders. Sometimes it is hard to distinguish between a full-fledged neurosis and a neurotic trait. Minor phobias are very common as are "conversion" symptoms which are a part of the condition known as hysteria. To classify these as a neurosis would depend on the degree of the condition. Alcoholism, drug addiction, and some sexual difficulties are sometimes classified as neuroses.

Self-therapy is likely to be easiest and most effective in changing our mental attitudes, character traits and our wrong patterns of thinking. Emotional illnesses may result from these and correcting them may bring relief from the illness.

Actual danger from self-help is minimal provided it is not attempted when the contraindications above are observed. Some precautions may be needed at times but there are simple safeguards which can be followed which will avoid any possible danger.

These safeguards will be described.

**Anxiety and fatigue.** With any form of emotional disturbance certain emotions, feelings and ways of thinking seem to be commonplace. Anxiety, in varying amounts, is almost certain to be present. Anxiety might be defined as a feeling of apprehension or a fear without any definitely known reason for it. Another common symptom is fatigue. Most emotionally disturbed people complain of fatigue and lack of energy. Even though sleep is normal, the person wakens in the morning feeling tired. There are really two kinds of fatigue: physical through exertion, and emotional or mental. Mental fatigue is not well understood but is commonly thought to come from too much mental activity and from the inability to solve our problems.

**Negativism.** A negative attitude seems to go hand in hand with emotional and neurotic difficulties. Everything is *I can't* instead of *I can.* I can't really means I don't want to. There is a feeling of hopelessness and helplessness. Expectation of the worst is quite likely to bring trouble, for it is a form of negative suggestion and the subconscious may then cause behavior which will bring trouble.

**Inferiority feelings.** Feelings of inferiority and insecurity are very common. To some degree such emotions are almost universal. Even the brash, cocky, self-assured individual may be showing these characteristics in an unconscious effort to cover up his real feelings of inferiority. This compensation is similar to the behavior of the bully, who actually is hiding his cowardice.

Many men of great wealth have such strong feelings of insecurity that they continue through life accumulating more money. The man worth a million dollars and financially secure must strive for another million. When he has this he must continue to add to it. Undoubtedly each of the very few billionaires in the world has very strong feelings of insecurity which drive him to further accumulations of wealth.

Quite a few people with emotional troubles find themselves unable to concentrate well. When they read or study, their thoughts jump from one thing to another and they cannot keep them on what they are doing. With lack of concentration you do not register what you read and then cannot recall it. This can make learning difficult and may affect your working efficiency also.

Another common symptom which is a part of insecurity is the inability or dislike of making decisions. If you make a decision perhaps it will be the wrong one, so you hesitate and avoid reaching a decision. Fear of failure is a related matter. If you do not try, you cannot fail. Disregarded is the fact that neither can you succeed without trying. The very word *try* implies failure. When you say "I'll try," you imply that you probably will not succeed.

**Immaturity.** Immaturity is another common matter. Much neurotic behavior and thinking is on a very immature basis. The immature person in some ways has not grown up and so does not face reality and cannot handle his problems in an adult way. On the other hand it would be hard to find anyone completely free of minor immaturities. Again, it is largely a matter of degree whether this is abnormal.

The person who is emotionally disturbed or who has frequent psychosomatic illnesses is likely to become very self-centered. He worries about his condition, and develops a habit of being very concerned and dwells on himself almost continually. He is too busy thinking about himself to pay much attention to others. Everyone has a degree of self-importance, of course, but such a person is a large capital I. This does not mean that he is selfish or egotistical. He may be very generous, if he happens to think about someone else at times. Usually he is too busy with thoughts about himself.

On pages 119-121 there is a "balance sheet" giving character traits which can be assessed as either liabilities or assets. Changing these liabilities to assets is an important part of self-help. Balancing assets and liabilities and seeing how your assets outweigh your liabilities will serve to give you a better view of yourself and help overcome the well-known "inferiority complex."

**Psychosomatic illness.** When it comes to psychosomatic illness, the value of self-treatment depends largely on the severity of the illness and on the personality of the individual. Drugs may be helpful and medical treatment is usually indicated even though you also resort to self-help. If treatment is being given by a psychologist or psychiatrist, self-therapy would not be advisable unless your therapist agrees to it.

Just what is a psychosomatic illness? Dr. J. A. Winter, in his book *The Origins of Illness and Anxiety* (Julian Press, New York), gives a very good definition. He says:

We define a psychosomatic disease as an illness with the following characteristics:

1. The disorder is one of function, rather than of structure, although structural changes (in the body) may occur later.
2. It is precipitated by an inadequate stimulus.
3. The response is not appropriate to the stimulus.
4. It is based on some past experience, usually painful.
5. It is based on fixed associations—a certain stimulus will almost always elicit an unvarying response.

6. There seems to be a lack of awareness of Here and Now; the patient's reactions seem to overlook or ignore the present-time situation in favor of some previously experienced one.

Such illnesses seem to stem from problem situations and from words rather than actual infections or injuries.

Most of us realize that illness may have psychological causes but we like to believe this is something which may be so with others but not with us. Ours must be organic. If our doctor tells us we have a psychosomatic illness we may even resent it and find the idea unacceptable, at least until it is confirmed by some other physician. Unfortunately, a few doctors without training in psychosomatics will feel unable to cope with such an illness and may dismiss the patient with such a remark as "It's all in your head." It may be from your emotions, but it is not imaginary and just in your head. A psychologically produced pain hurts just as much as an organic one.

When patients are referred to me with this type of ailment they frequently will remark, "I don't know why Dr. Jones asked me to see you. You are a psychologist and my headache (or asthma, or what not) is a physical condition."

With an explanation of how our emotions and the subconscious mind can affect us, I find it valuable to explain the pendulum responses to questions and then to ask with pendulum answers, "Is there some emotional or psychological reason for your headaches?" When the referring physician's diagnosis of a psychosomatic condition is correct, the answer with the pendulum is invariably *yes*. This is then accepted by the patient. I have not told him it is so—he had told me. His subconscious has confirmed it. Acceptance of the idea on his part is the first step forward in treatment.

Since the reader may not be familiar with the conditions which physicians usually consider as psychosomatic, a number of the more common ones are listed here. To include all would be like printing a large part of a medical dictionary. With some, such as allergy and arthritis, so little is known about them that the picture is confusing. There may be only an organic basis but usually there are psychological causes, hence these are included in the list.

Some of the illnesses classified as psychosomatic are as follows:

*Respiratory system.* Allergy, sinusitis, hay fever, common cold, bronchitis, asthma, emphysema, pulmonary tuberculosis.

*Skin.* Eczema, urticaria, hives and many other skin conditions, some classed as allergies.

*Digestive.* Obesity, constipation, colitis, diarrhea, peptic ulcer, vomiting, oesophagal spasm, lack of appetite in some conditions, hemorrhoids, gall-bladder disease.

*Vascular.* High blood pressure, coronary heart disease, paroxysmal tachycardia (sudden rapid heart beat), Reynaud's disease, Buerger's disease.

*Urinary.* Enuresis (bed wetting), nervous frequency, urgency and incontinence, postoperative urinary retention.

*Nervous system, endocrine.* Tic douloureux, trigeminal neuralgia, migraine, hiccups, drug addiction, alcoholism, some forms of epilepsy, possibly Parkinsonism, multiple sclerosis, myasthenia gravis, hyperthyroidism, diabetes mellitus, goiter, hypoglycemia.

*Genital. Male*—impotence, premature ejaculation, infertility. *Female*—Many menstrual disturbances particularly dysmenorrhea (cramps), infertility, habitual abortion, frigidity, possibly leucorrhea, trichomonas vaginitis, dyspareunia.

Stress and tension may serve to lower bodily resistance so that we become more susceptible to even infectious diseases and in this sense it could be said that all illness has an emotional background.

## SUMMARY

We are not concerned here with the very serious, major emotional diseases—the neuroses and insanity. Self-help would probably be of small value with them and psychiatric or psychological help is required. One point is important here. A person who is quite disturbed and realizes that some of his behavior is compulsive and irrational may wonder if he is psychotic—insane in ordinary terms. This may be a source of much worry and more disturbance. It is very unlikely, though some who are "off their rocker" may have some realization of it. If this is a worry, a psychiatrist certainly should be consulted for a diagnosis.

Anxiety, fatigue, negativism, inferiority feelings, worry, inability to concentrate, difficulty in making decisions, immaturity, and self-centeredness usually accompany minor disturbances. These are neurotic sysmptoms but would not class as neuroses. They may accompany an actual neurosis. Of course there are other neurotic traits. There will be further discussion of many of these matters.

The more common psychosomatic illnesses have been listed. It is well to be aware of these in case you ever develop one of them. They may need medical treatment, but certainly psychological treament is also necessary.

# Chapter 8

# THE VALUE OF POSITIVE THINKING AND HEALTHFUL RELAXATION

There are few people whose thinking patterns and ways of behaving are such that improving them is unnecessary. Undoubtedly some of yours could be changed to your advantage. Emotions, conditioned reflexes and your training in childhood lead to these patterns. Some of the matters discussed in this chapter may not apply to you, but almost certainly you will find others that do. They can be changed if you will follow the methods given here. And the changes certainly will make you happier with yourself and more successful.

Are you a negative thinker? In general, a well-adjusted person tends to think in a positive way. He will have a reasonably correct view of himself. He will also realize his lack of some abilities but he directs his efforts into channels where his talents can be used. Those he lacks do not bother him and he disregards them. He is an optimist, establishes goals, and believes he can reach them. Usually he does. With positive thinking his subconscious mind leads him to perform and behave so that he does the things necessary to succeed reasonably well and to enjoy good health. He tends most of the time to be happy and to enjoy life. When things do not go just as he wishes, it does not upset him greatly. His neurotic symptoms will be few.

Negative thinking has the opposite effect. The end result is unhappiness, worry, anxiety, frustration, and hostility. Conflicts produce these emotions and the negative thinker is more subject to emotional illness. He does not like to face reality. He fears to set goals because he anticipates failure, and he is not likely to be very successful. His feelings of inferiority are like a ball and chain on his foot. His subconsciously controlled behavior will probably bring failure.

A number of books have been written about the value of positive thinking. All aim at the same thing but approach it from different directions. For the person who is strongly religious, Peale's *Power of Positive Thinking* (Prentice-Hall, Inc., Englewood Cliffs, New Jersey) is excellent. Here the approach is through prayer and belief that divine help can be obtained. Other books have also stressed this. The writings of Emmett Fox earlier in the century are of great value. This is true as well for those of Harold Sherman, *Your Key to Happiness* (Putnam, New York) and others.

A metaphysical approach along the lines of Oriental philosophies is that of U.S. Andersen (*The Secret of Secrets*, Nelson, New York). The methods of developing positive thinking which he advocates can be most helpful.

A matter-of-fact, common sense view is that of the late Claude Bristol in *The Magic of Believing* (Prentice-Hall, Inc., Englewood Cliffs, New Jersey). Bristol offers ways of influencing the subconscious to cause us to act so that we reach our goals. His methods are practical and will bring results, as will those of other writers on the subject.

Since whole books have dealt with this subject and the ways to develop positive thinking, we can only consider this briefly here. Everyone would find it of real value to read one of these books and then to apply the methods which are given.

The real secret in thinking positively is belief. It is not easy to change the habit of negative thinking, but it can be accomplished. No one can think positively at all times, but it can be developed into a habit so that it is done most of the time. Such thinking is no magic wand to get us out of our difficulties instantly. Determination and patience are needed, with much practice of whatever techniques are used to produce positive thinking habits. Some little time may pass before results come and discouragement slows the process.

Positive habits of thinking will be of great help in

changing character traits and attitudes, in helping you find success and happiness and in relieving illness. In the matter of illness, every physician knows the mental attitude of a patient is vitally important. If he is pessimistic and has no expectation of getting well, no will to live, he well may die. On the other hand, a very ill person with a strong urge to live, and who thinks he will recover, probably will get well.

**How our fears affect us.** Negativism is a conditioned reflex. Our fear-based emotions spring from past conditioning, negative thinking being a large factor in producing fears. These emotions are fear itself, anxiety, frustration, hostility and guilt, with nervous tension accompanying them.

Fear itself is consciously recognized. We know we are afraid of some definite object or situation. We may know why we are afraid of it. The causes of a phobia may not be consciously known. They seldom are. Fear of death is one rather common fear. Even religious people who believe in a future life may have strong fears of death. Possibly this comes from the fact that some religions teach the idea of hell-fire and damnation too strongly in an effort to frighten people into being good.

Fear of death may be aroused by the conditioning we have undergone when loved ones have passed away, perhaps painfully. Often the fear is not so much of death itself as of suffering greatly at the time of death.

Fear of illness also springs from conditioning, as do all fears. As we mature, most of us contract some of the childhood diseases and witness the illnesses of others. No one likes to be ill. At least consciously we do not want this. Our fears of illness may be about ourselves or those we love. Health fads, indicating the extent of such fears, are common. The cost of pills and medications taken to prevent disease runs into many millions annually.

Another common and quite natural fear is that concerning finances. The struggle to make a living is not easy; it is particularly difficult to gain real financial security. Lack of this promotes continual fear or apprehension.

Insecurity is not only a result of lack of money but may involve personal relationships, fear of not being loved or of rejection. One of our strongest unconscious drives is to be loved. If we are rejected frequently as we mature, this need becomes stronger, as a neurotic symptom. With negative thinking we expect to be rejected. One may become so fearful of being repulsed that an inability to love develops and love cannot be accepted because rejection is thought sure to follow.

Anxiety is a form of fear, sometimes a general feeling of something unpleasant about to happen. An anxious individual usually is unable to tell why he feels anxious. The fears behind it are subconscious and unrecognized. Anxiety is a most uncomfortable emotion. The most common of all neuroses is what is termed an anxiety state, with anxiety so great that panic attacks occur.

When there seems to be no definite reason for anxiety, it has been called "free floating anxiety." This is based on a fear that something unpleasant or horrible is going to happen. It is as if the sword of Damocles hangs over one and may fall at any moment. Any unpleasant happening or any failure is a confirmation of the fear and the conviction of more to come is stronger. The expectation of disaster is a conditioned reflex. The well-adjusted person lacks such expectations and is not disturbed when things do not go right. He shrugs it off and proceeds on his way, although he may not like it.

With this type of anxiety, the sufferer is unable to take any action to escape from his apprehension. There is nothing he can do about it, he feels. Hopelessness is then felt. Inability to take action causes more anxiety. Tension becomes chronic. If the person could escape, anxiety would be allayed but it persists because he cannot get away.

**Hostility and anger.** Anger and hostility are related emotions. They are entirely normal emotions when they do not become too strong or too prolonged. You would not be a human being if, at times, you did not become angry and if you never developed feelings of hostility towards others, or towards fate, or even toward yourself. Naturally these emotions must be controlled. You cannot strike out when angry or you would frequently be in trouble—the other fellow might be bigger than you are!

Many people regard these emotions as "bad" and may have strong guilt when they are experienced. Guilt may call subconsciously for self-punishment. Such an emotion will then be stifled and suppressed the moment it is stimulated because it is wrong to have it. Another reason for suppression is fear of loss of control in anger and the possible results if not controlled. The combination of guilt and suppression can bring unpleasant consequences such as migraine headaches and other painful symptoms. When anger and hostility are viewed as normal emo-

tional responses to stimuli they do not require suppression.
Bottling them up does not discharge the emotions. They
persist and bubble away under the surface in the subconscious. The proper handling of such emotions is to
discharge them in some acceptable way. There are several
acceptable ways. Too often suppressed hostility is "projected" onto someone else, on those nearest us who may
not in any way be the cause of the hostility. Husband or
wife, or the children may bear the brunt of the hostility,
often shown by irritability.

With anger controlled, it can sometimes be talked out.
It is not necessary to quarrel, to swear, to be sarcastic
and hostile. Talking in a calm way about the situation or
about the person provoking the hostility will nullify the
emotion.

Another way of discharging such feeling is through
exercise. How much satisfaction there is for the golfer in
hitting a long drive with all his strength; for the tennis
player in "smacking" that ball hard. The baseball player
enjoys batting a home run. In many sports the player is
working off his latent hostilities without realizing it. He
feels very good thereafter. Any form of exercise, chopping
wood, working in the garden, calisthenics, all serve to
discharge latent hostility or that which is being experienced at the time. The baseball fan is working off his hostilities when he shouts, "kill the umpire!" or badgers some
player.

A psychological law is that a stronger emotion will always nullify a weaker one. Strong anger may overcome
fear and the angered person may attack the one frightening him. If fear is greater than anger, it will prevail and
there would be avoidance instead of attack. It is not easy
to summon up a stronger emotion when we are angry,
but it is possible. It is easier to overcome hostility, which
is not as strong as anger. If a man is angry at his wife,
controls it and seizes her in a laughing way and kisses her
instead of berating her, the anger will disappear. The
emotions of love and desire will take over. If she is angry
too, hers will also vanish—provided her anger is not too
great.

There is another technique of value in many situations,
including when anger is stimulated. Again, there must be
control first. When angry or upset in any way, think to
yourself the phrases "So what? What of it? It doesn't
matter." With a little practice and with acceptance of the
idea involved in these phrases the emotion dwindles away

and has no effect. If your feelings are hurt, if you are frustrated, in any unsetting situation, saying these phrases to yourself will ease things. The emotions aroused run off your back like water off a duck instead of sinking in and bothering you. Practicing this when disturbed will be found to be of real value. Of course if this were overdone one might become too indifferent, but properly handled it is most effective.

**Frustration.** Life is full of frustrations. Beginning in infancy we encounter these with parental prohibitions. "No," "You must not do that," and other negations are heard from our earliest years. The "I want" runs headlong into the "You can't" of society. The prohibitions of parents and of society are necessary but they are frustrating and the basis of conflict.

In later life some of our desires and needs are not fulfilled either—more frustration. It is a natural emotion and only when it is chronic is it serious. This phrase, "So what?" can be a good way of discharging feelings of frustration, helping us tolerate the situations provoking frustration. Those who have goals and accomplish them adjust well to frustrations when they fail to reach some other goal. Continual failure may bring chronic frustration and its end results.

If our primary needs in life are filled fairly adequately, frustrations are tolerated with no difficulty. We need to love and be loved; to have a good relationship with our family. We must have self-respect and see ourselves with a proper viewpoint, maintaining a good image of ourselves. There must be self-reliance and self-confidence so that we can be reasonably successful. We must have goals toward which we work, including the personal and the financial. With accomplishment along these lines, good mental (and probably physical) health will follow.

**Guilt.** We all have faults and weaknesses and fall short of our ideals. No one is perfect. There is something of the caveman in all of us, instincts or attitudes suppressed by the taboos of society. At times we do things which we regret, have thoughts which we regard as bad. This is a part of human nature. Conscience is a brake on many of our desires, fortunately, or the world would be a much worse place than it is. However we can be entirely too conscientious. We should learn from our mistakes and our wrong doing and wrong thinking. We should try not to repeat something conscience says is wrong. Dwelling on the past and developing strong feelings of guilt is most harmful. Guilt and shame can take quite a toll, with self-punishment and emotional disturbance resulting. Of course one of the greatest sources of guilt is in the sphere of sex, to be discussed later.

The end product of the basic fear emotions and accompanying stress is nervous tension. This may be evidenced by nervous habits such as biting the finger nails, restlessness, smoking, too much drinking, and a host of other symptoms.

**Worry.** Worry is another most unpleasant conditioned reflex, when overdone. Everyone worries at times and it is a normal emotion in some situations, as when a loved one is seriously ill. Chronic worry is abnormal. The "worry wart" worries no matter how well things are going. If the cause for some worry is ended, he quickly finds something else to worry about. Instead of resting, he lies awake nights with his mind concentrating on worries. He would deny it, but he probably derives pleasure and satisfaction from worrying. In this case it is masochistic and he is punishing himself.

What else promotes chronic worry? Identification may be a factor and, if one of the parents was a chronic worrier, this habit may develop from dramatizing oneself as that parent, unconsciously trying to be like the father or mother. My impression is that women are much more likely to be chronic worriers than men. The object of identification is usually the mother, but it well could be the father, or any close relative.

The main basis of worry is negativism and apprehension, always expecting the worst to befall. The result of worry is tension, thus increasing the tendency to worry—a vicious circle.

The chronic worrier must exert considerable effort to overcome the habit, particularly if masochism is involved. He must break any identification by realizing he is copying someone else's behavior pattern. Every time he finds himself worrying, he should divert his mind to pleasant things. Another method of breaking any habit is that advocated by the late Knight Dunbar, who was the greatest authority on habits and their formation. Dunbar pointed out that trying hard to break a habit, trying to desist from it, only reinforces it—again that old demon, the law of reversed effect. He advocated visualizing the end result (a form of suggestion). Greatly exaggerating the habit whenever it is being evidenced helps to break it.

Carrying out this last idea in the case of worry could

be accomplished by thinking the very worst and making a deliberate effort to worry. You could think to yourself, "I really must worry hard now; what I am worrying about is terrible. What is going to happen is going to be awful!" Soon the situation will become completely ridiculous and you may find yourself seeing it as humorous and laughable.

Often the chronic worrier says, "I try but I just can't stop worrying." A negative thought, but what he actually means is that he doesn't want to stop worrying. *I can't* always means *I don't want to.* This is a good thing to remember when the thought comes into your mind. Perhaps the reason for not wanting to stop is a fear of some kind, or enjoyment in what the worrier is doing.

**Jealousy and envy.** These are somewhat related emotions, both stemming from feelings of inferiority and insecurity. A person who feels secure in accepting love and who trusts the loved one will never feel jealous unless there is proof of betrayal. Jealousy stems from uncertainty about oneself and a feeling of unworthiness.

This emotion takes different forms, jealousy of an actual preferred rival being one. In this case it centers on the rival and the feeling may be warranted. Showing jealousy to the object of one's affection is apt to be a fatal mistake. In such a situation about all one can do is to make the best of it, refusing to be affected. Using the "so what" technique can develop an armor so the pain of the emotion will run off rather than sink in.

Jealousy can be merely vague, without a definite object. Here, there is fear and anticipation. The jealous person is afraid someone will appear on the scene who will supersede him, or that there may be a rival of whom he is unaware. Distrust of the object of his affection is involved. Love without trust will never have a successful outcome, and there is trouble ahead. Extreme jealousy is probably paranoid, as in the case described where the husband tried to uncover his wife's infidelity by questioning her under hypnosis.

Envy is a more normal emotion than jealousy, but is again based on feelings of insecurity and inferiority. It would be directed against a rival in other fields than love, such as in business, or against the possessor of any coveted advantage or object.

**Relaxation.** Accompanying nervous tension is inability to relax. Many people are quite unable to relax—they simply don't know how. Chronic tension is most detrimental, both physically and mentally, and often is a main cause in producing psychosomatic illness, stomach ulcers being one example. Relaxation tends to discharge nervous tension, at least temporarily. With practice in relaxation, chronic tension can be overcome to a large extent.

Entire books have been written showing how to relax. Best known of these is Jacobson's *You Must Relax* (Whittlesey House, New York). Jacobson called his method "progressive relaxation," and it does teach how to relax. Unfortunately, several weeks of continued practice are required to learn it well. A much simpler and even more effective method is available which can be learned in three or four trials, but it is almost unknown.

This technique was described by Frederick Pierce in his book *Mobilizing the Mid-Brain* (Putnam & Sons, New York), a self-help book of considerable value published in 1924. It is now out of print but can be obtained sometimes in used-book stores.

Pierce called his relaxation exercise *decubitis*. It is based on a sound principle which he discovered. One day, when bowling, his arm had become tired. While resting the ball on the rack, his attention was distracted to something else and when he started to pick up the ball his fingers slipped from the holes. The fatigued muscles had relaxed completely. When he tried consciously to let his arm relax the muscles did not loosen so much. Experimenting, he developed his exercise based on this principle. If a group of muscles, such as an arm or a leg, is tired, distraction of attention from them brings automatically complete relaxation of these muscles.

**How to relax.** To accomplish complete body relaxation with this method it is best to be lying down. It can be carried out in a sitting position, though not as completely. Six exercises are involved. The first is best performed in a sitting position on a bed, then lying back as soon as it has been carried out. Close your eyes and let your neck and shoulders be as loose as possible. Then rotate your head four times, very slowly, in a clockwise circle, trying to let the muscles loosen still more. Then reverse the movement, making it counterclockwise for four revolutions.

As soon as this is completed, you should lie back and immediately raise your right foot about twelve inches from the bed. Make the muscles as stiff and taut as possible so they will tire quicker. As you hold the leg elevated, begin thinking of the muscles, following them from the toes right up to the hip. The eyes should be closed through the entire series of exercises. You visualize the muscles in your "mind's eye." By this means you have distracted your attention from the neck and shoulder muscles, so they will automatically relax completely.

Keep the leg elevated until it is thoroughly tired and it becomes an effort to hold it up. This may take from one minute to three or four. When it feels very tired do not lower it slowly—let it drop heavily, completely limp. This may take some practice to make it quite limp as it falls. The instant the right leg has fallen, raise the left one in the same manner, stiffening it. Immediately divert your thoughts to this leg, again following the muscles from the toes to the hip. Depending on the time it takes to tire the leg muscles, you may have to go back over the muscles in your thoughts two or three times, doing it very slowly. Then the leg is allowed to fall.

The right arm should immediately be raised into a Nazi salute position, but with clenched fist. Stiffen and tighten the muscles to tire them more quickly. Follow in your thoughts the muscles from the fingertips up to the shoulder and neck, repeating as often as necessary until the arm is quite tired. As arms are lighter than legs, it will take longer to tire them. As with the legs, the tired arm should be allowed to fall by your side as limp as the proverbial dishrag. The left arm is then exercised in the same way, the thoughts instantly diverted when the right one falls.

When the left arm has fallen, your thoughts can be diverted from it by imagining, with your eyes still closed, a circle on the ceiling above you. Imagine it to be about four feet in diameter. Follow this circle around clockwise with your eyes. Then reverse it and go counter-clockwise four times. This should be done slowly. Completing this, visualize a square instead, with sides about four feet long. Go around it in the same way, four times clockwise and four times counter-clockwise.

This completes the six exercises. You should then lie for a few moments enjoying the relaxation you have established. Divert your mind from the eyes by thinking of anything pleasant. Proficiency with this will come in three or four experiences with it and you will be surprised at the degree of relaxation achieved.

**How to use this relaxation method.** In order to learn the method, it should be done at least once a day for two weeks. It can be performed later whenever tension has developed. You are conditioning yourself to remain more relaxed during your daily life and will soon notice this effect. Of course situations which promote tension will arise but you will be much more relaxed between such times. Tension will no longer be chronic. You will retain nervous habits unless they are broken in some way, but they may be modified somewhat. Learning relaxation will also enable you to become a better subject for auto-hypnosis.

As I have given it, this exercise is modified slightly from Pierce's description. He recommends lowering the arms and legs very slowly, instead of dropping them suddenly. In my experience dropping them is best, but you might experiment and find which is best in your own case.

**Deep breathing to relieve tensions.** Another technique helpful in overcoming nervous tension is the practice of deep breathing. Health faddists have long stressed its value but few of us take the trouble to try it. It can be combined very nicely with the Pierce method of relaxation, performed just before, while sitting up.

Yoga practitioners have found breathing exercises of great value. They believe them to be of utmost importance in maintaining health. Such exercises have been evolved over a period of 2000 years or more. Many are complicated and students are warned of danger in them, urging that they be performed only with the guidance of a teacher. One simple exercise is very effective and without danger if not overdone.

This has been termed the 4–8–4 exercise. In performing it you should sit in a relaxed position but with the body erect, shoulders back, and head erect. The left arm should be relaxed at your side or with the hand in your lap. If you are left-handed this should be the position of the right arm. Lift the other hand to your face, fingers together but thumb extended. Press the thumb against the right nostril, closing that side of the nose and inhale through the left, taking in a full breath. This should take about four seconds. You can time it by counting slowly "a thousand one, a thousand two" and on to a thousand four.

Now hold your breath, counting in the same way to eight. While doing so, remove your thumb from the right side of the nose, moving the hand so the forefinger closes the left nostril. When the count of eight is completed, exhale through the right nostril slowly to a count of four, being sure to empty the lungs.

Keeping the left nostril still closed, breathe in again

through the right to the count of four, filling the lungs. Shift the hand, closing the right nostril and freeing the left. Hold the breath again for eight counts and exhale through the left side of the nose to the count of four. This completes a cycle.

The exercise should include four such cycles at first. It would be well to use this on arising in the morning, and again in the evening. If done only once a day it will be found very beneficial. With some experience with the exercise, the number of cycles should be increased to six. Still later you might try eight, but if you become somewhat dizzy, cut down the number of cycles.

**Yoga and your health.** Such breathing fills you with oxygen and clears your lungs. A feeling of well-being follows. You feel much more relaxed and also energetic. Results are well worthwhile and only a few moments are required for the exercise. Some patients have told me they seem to have less anxiety for some time following its performance. In my opinion, it is of value in some psychosomatic illnesses such as in asthma and bronchitis. Of course it could be done by an asthmatic only when his breathing difficulty is not too great, certainly not during an attack.

Yogins used the term *prana* for life force or primal energy and believe with this exercise that a fresh supply of *prana* is accumulated in the tissue and lungs. Oxygen is a part of *prana*. In theory this stimulates the entire nervous system, the body and the senses.

Yoga teaches a way of healing based on intensive concentration (developed only with much practice), and then the use of autosuggestion, following this breathing exercise. However, the exercise is continued to a point of heavy perspiration and exhaustion. It is supposed to be done in the sunlight, and also in the water while bathing, and with much repetition.

## SUMMARY

A better understanding of your emotions and a different viewpoint towards some of them should be helpful to you. You can learn to modify and control them. Self-hypnosis and autosuggestion will aid greatly in this.

As you practice self-hypnosis you will almost certainly find that you are more relaxed and free of tension during your daily life. But if you have much difficulty relaxing you should practice the Pierce method. In turn this will help you to go deeper into hypnosis. In fact, this method of relaxation has been used as a method of inducing hypnosis. When it is practiced some people find themselves spontaneously in hypnosis when they have concluded the exercise. Adding some suggestions to it will increase the tendency.

If you will take the time to practice the yoga breathing exercise once each day, or better twice, you will soon notice that you are feeling much better and more energetic. It acts to promote good health and is certainly worth the few moments of time needed to go through it.

*Chapter 9*

# HOW TO OVERCOME
# FEELINGS OF INFERIORITY
# AND A POVERTY "COMPLEX"

Few people are without some feelings of inferiority. It is surprising to find so many who feel themselves most unworthy and inferior. Such feelings are a tremendous handicap. In all probability you have some such feelings, perhaps mild, possibly strong. A part of your program should be to rid yourself of them. Frequently they prevent one from attempting to do things which he is quite capable of doing.

Feelings of inferiority are based on conditioned reflexes and result in a wrong view of self which may cause many difficulties. A poverty complex is closely related to inferiority feelings.

In his self-help book, *Psycho-Cybernetics* (Prentice-Hall, Inc., Englewood Cliffs, New Jersey), Dr. Maltz lays great stress on what he terms the responsibility for emotional troubles on wrong conceptions about yourself. Correcting these views will overcome the emotional problems.

Dr. Rolf Alexander, in *Creative Realism* (Pageant Press, New York) says almost the same thing in describing "false personality." Bringing out the real personality eliminates many problems.

Much can be accomplished by changing your self-evaluation. You are what you think you are, and your subconscious carries out the ideas you have about yourself.

If you expect to fail or doubt your success, the law of reversed effect will bring failure. It is vitally important to see yourself correctly. As the old philosophers have said, "Know Thyself." "Knowledge is power" is another very true adage.

**Do you have physical disabilities?** Among other reasons for this inferiority bugaboo is physical appearance. Dr. Maltz is a plastic surgeon and he stresses the importance that appearance has with us. Ugly features can be a great trial, as can deformities of any kind. Dr. Maltz cites many cases where correction of these conditions by surgery brought great changes of personality. A feeling of humiliation may accompany any deformity, such, as perhaps, a harelip. A congenital deformity can be a great source of self-consciousness and feelings of inferiority. Some individuals who have been maimed in accidents may hold these feelings, too.

Many people have little or no sense of personal worth due to physical defects. Examples of these are hearing loss, bad vision, speech impediments, obesity, very short stature, etc. If defects are of psychological origin, as may be the case, they can be helped—obesity, for instance. If the defects are such that little or nothing can be done, however, personality difficulties may result. In this case, the person needs to correct his view of himself as a person of worth. When he can gain a healthy liking and respect for himself, the attitude of others towards him will reflect his own opinion. We need to realize that others think of us much as we think of ourselves. If one can lose his concern about his defects, they will be of no importance to anyone. A man of short stature, as an example, should realize that quality is much more important than quantity. It is well to remember that your true friends will pay no heed to any defect you may have.

Everyone instinctively wishes to be loved and appreciated. The person who is physically beautiful or handsome is often so wrapped up in himself as to be unable to give love or to have regard for others. One who has warmth and appreciation for others is a magnetic, attractive person, regardless of physical attributes or defects. A woman who is less than beautiful in her own eyes should be aware of the case of George Sand, noted French writer. This woman had so much warmth and personal magnetism that young men fell in love with her when she was in her sixties and seventies. Yet she was "horse-faced" and very homely.

Few people thought of F.D.R., crippled by polio, as being unable to walk, because the man's personality was "bigger than life." He was loved by a majority of people. Helen Keller, blind all her life, rose above her great handicap and is another example of a person who lived most successfully despite her condition. These people evaluated themselves properly.

The need here is for genuine self-respect. Self-hypnosis and suggestion can be of great benefit under these circumstances in attaining better self-evaluation.

**A disability needn't keep you out of the swim.** A friend of mine was an exceptionally good swimmer and enjoyed it greatly. On a hunting trip one day, he stumbled over a shotgun and fell. The gun discharged and blew his hand off at the wrist. For some years after recovery, he would not enter the water at any public place, feeling conspicuous with his hand amputated. On a trip where we had an opportunity to swim at a fine Pacific beach, I took him to task and pointed out how ridiculous it was to feel so humiliated and so conscious of his arm. What if the hand was missing? It was the result of an unfortunate accident. He could swim just as well and no one would pay any particular attention to him. Obviously he had a fine athletic body. He was depriving himself of much pleasure and it was time to view the situation more correctly. He listened to my scolding, laughed and said, "I guess I've been a fool. Let's go in." After this he took up the sport again.

**Proper suggestions bring perfect figures.** Some years ago it was stylish for women to have small breasts. Those with larger ones bound them tightly to be fashionable. Today the situation is reversed and many girls wish to be a Sophia Loren. A flat-chested girl is extremely sensitive about her lack of development. This is such a common situation that "falsies" are sold in huge numbers, greatly deceiving the male sex. Several plastic surgeons deal almost exclusively with this problem and have busy practices. They operate, placing a piece of plastic material behind the breast, building it up to the desired size. Other plastic surgeons claim possible danger from such an operation and refuse to perform it. But girls flock to those who do.

Strangely, many could have this accomplished, or possibly accomplish it themselves, without the necessity of surgery. Breast development by hypnotic suggestion has been reported in many instances, and of seven cases among my own patients, six found an increase in measurement of from one and a half inches to more than two inches. To say that these girls were pleased is putting it mildly.

This was carried out by the use of straight verbal suggestion, plus the use of visual imagery. The girls were instructed to close their eyes on going to bed at night and to form an image of themselves as they wished their breasts to be.

Another suggestion was also used. Before reaching puberty a girl has no breasts. At puberty they begin to develop, but sometimes the process stops before the breasts reach a satisfactory size. This was stated as an obvious fact and it was suggested that the subconscious mind would now stimulate the same process of growth again, just as it had at the time puberty was beginning. Growth would continue until the breasts had increased at least an inch and a half. It was mentioned that various endocrinal, hormonal and other physiological processes were involved when the breasts first began to develop and the same processes would begin again. Whether or not this actually resulted, I cannot say. Judging from the growth that did occur, it may have happened.

A GIRL WHO REJECTED FEMININITY. The one case where there was failure was a girl who completely rejected femininity. She did not wish to be a girl, she wanted to be a man. As a matter of fact, all six of the others had the same resentment at being female, though to a much less degree. Some effort was made to change this attitude. Whether this may have had something to do in stimulating the breast development, I don't know, though it is worth following up. Perhaps in rejecting femininity as a child, the inner mind carries out the idea and the breasts do not fully develop. But this is conjecture.

Dr. Cheek, a gynecologist, has found rejection of femininity an important cause of many female ailments, including infertility, habitual abortion (miscarriage), menopausal troubles and others. This is of course related to self-imagery. He has found a change of viewpoint towards the self has helped many of his patients overcome these conditions.

A woman's desire to be a male is sometimes caused by the woman as a child hearing her parents say they wanted a boy. A brother may be much more favored during childhood and this can cause a desire in his sister to be a boy so she will receive the same attention and favors. Another more adult reason is envy of the position

of the male in our society, with the advantages to men
in life. Of course, homosexuality may even be involved.

How much better for a woman to have hypnotic suggestion rather than submit to a dangerous operation for
breast development. My patients used autosuggestion as
a supplement to treatment. While I have no evidence that
development can be accomplished entirely through autosuggestion, I would be greatly surprised if it could not.
It would best be done under self-hypnosis. No possible
harm could come from attempting this and I am quite sure
many girls would produce measurable results—literally!
It should be well worth the time and effort for the flat-
chested girl. My six patients ranged in age from twenty-
two to thirty years old.

Whether or not any other part of the body could be
affected through suggestion is not known. Hypnosis is not
a magic wand, nor can it work miracles. Again, no harm
would follow from trying, but changing such parts as
thick, heavy ankles or legs would seem most unlikely.

**How inferiority feelings are developed in childhood.** It
is in our early years that inferiority feelings begin to develop. Parents often expect entirely too much of their off-
spring, and failures may be scolded and reproached. Junior
is expected to be a genius like his father and mother.
Then the child becomes afraid to try for fear he will fail
and this would bring more reproaches down on his head.
We should learn from our failures and then we may succeed the next time we try. Being scolded or punished for
failure blocks the incentive to try again.

Just as harmful for the child is the overprotective parent. With love and a desire to help our little darlings, we
sometimes do not let them do things for themselves so
they may learn. With little opportunity to solve problems
by their own efforts, how can they learn the way to do
things? As a parent myself, I know how often I am
tempted to "help" and how hard it often is to refrain. I
have on occasion been brought up by the remark, "Let
*me* do it Daddy!," a very appropriate one

Some alcoholics seem to be the spoiled brats of childhood. Everything was done for them by overprotective
and overindulgent parents. They have never learned to
do things for themselves. When grown and this becomes
necessary, they cannot face reality and alcohol serves as
an escape.

Still another situation is the younger child, particularly
when the elder is of the same sex. In trying to compete

with an older brother there are few ways in which the younger child can succeed. With encouragement and explanations that he is not expected to do as much, he can adjust and not lose confidence in himself and his abilities.

Few parents are authorities on child-raising and child psychology. As parents we will make mistakes. Indeed, child psychologists sometimes have children who are badly spoiled. Sometimes it is easy to tell someone else what to do, hard to do it yourself.

Careless remarks made by parents to their children can at times be picked up by the subconscious and will become fixed ideas which later are carried out like posthypnotic suggestions. They are more likely to become fixed if the child is under an emotion, perhaps when being punished. Suggestibility is then increased.

Telling an offending child, "You're a bad boy," may sound trivial. Heard again and again, he may accept the idea and compulsively be bad. Probably he has been a naughty boy, not a bad one. Bad means evil. With adults I have frequently found similar statements which have been pounded into the subconscious. "You're worthless." "You'll never amount to anything." "You never do as you're told." "You're just a little rebel." "When I tell you to do something, you always do just the opposite." "You're stupid."

A STRANGE COMPULSION IS SUCCESSFULLY TREATED. Some of these last phrases played a part in a rather strange situation where a young man came to me feeling quite desperate. He told me he needed psychiatric help badly and had gone to five different psychiatrists, making one visit to each.

He said, "I have a compulsion to do everything the opposite from what I'm told to do, particularly if told in any sort of positive or commanding way. Fortunately I inherited money and don't have to work as I doubt if I could hold a job. When I went to these psychiatrists and they had taken a case history, each one ended by saying 'Come back next week' or some such remark. Then I can't go back. It's impossible! What am I going to do? Can you break this with hypnosis?"

I told the young fellow I did not know but we could see what could be done. How to hypnotize him was a problem. Weighing every word, I said, "How can I possibly hypnotize you? It's impossible—you can't be hypnotized. I would want you to feel a heaviness coming into your eyelids and to have you soon close them, but I notice that they are wide open and instead of getting heavy, they are undoubtedly getting lighter and lighter, and wider and wider open. Instead of relaxing as you should to enter hypnosis, you are sitting there getting more and more rigid, stiffening yourself. I can see how tense you are. You can't possibly be hypnotized when you are so tense. Instead of feeling a bit drowsy and listless, you are becoming wider and wider awake."

I continued further along this line, saying exactly the opposite of what I intended, and in a few moments he had responded by going into a deep hypnotic state. I was then able to bring out some of the reasons for his rebellion and negativism. They traced back to such remarks as have been mentioned, spoken by an irritable, dominating father and accompanied by much punishment. This was the key, although other causes were also involved. Subsequently he was able to visit a psychiatrist for further work, as his case was not of a kind which I take.

Similar reactions, though nothing as severe as this, are not infrequent. Dr. Clark Hull at Yale conducted many scientific experiments with hypnosis. One test of hypnotizability is to have a subject stand in front of the operator and then suggest that the subject will fall backwards. When this is done, Hull found that about one subject in twenty would fall forward instead.

**The poverty complex and what to do about it.** Closely related to the inferiority complex is its cousin, the poverty complex. Perhaps the word complex should be defined, for it is used glibly by many without knowing its meaning. A complex is an emotionally charged group of related ideas, feelings, memories and impulses working together, mainly in the subconscious.

Inferiority and poverty often act together, holding one back from success. Much more is heard of the former, but the latter is common, too.

To illustrate this, Philip D. is a lawyer and a good one. With a fine professional reputation and a fairly good practice, he should have had a good income, but until recently it amounted to only a few thousand a year, after deduction of overhead expenses. Because he thought in small terms—dimes instead of dollars—a small fee was often his charge where a much larger one would have been reasonable. In one of his cases he had saved a corporation more than a hundred thousand dollars but had collected only fifteen hundred for his work. It was his largest fee until then.

A psychologist managed to show him how his poverty complex was affecting him. Its roots went back to childhood. He had to contribute to the family's support from an early age, first delivering newspapers and doing odd jobs. There always was a lack of money. His clothes were often hand-me-downs from an older brother. Even food was sometimes a problem in the home. Phil was ambitious. With the aid of a loan from a relative and by working, he had made his way through college and law school.

When all these contributing factors had been realized and he saw how his behavior was motivated by them, Phil had little trouble changing and his income quickly increased to what it should previously have been. He re-evaluated himself and his worth.

**How to conquer the "gambling fever."** A very detrimental neurotic symptom which may develop from the inferiority complex is compulsive gambling. The extent of this is evidenced by the enormous sums staked at the various racetracks about the country, at the Nevada gaming tables, and in illegal gambling of many types. The profits to the gambling fraternity run into hundreds of millions. No figures are available, of course, for most gambling is illegal and either unknown to authorities or privately condoned.

The old saying, "horse players die broke," is a truism and has few exceptions. It is "the house," the gambling syndicates, the professionals, who win. Even aware that the odds are all against him, the gambler compulsively continues to lose.

Compulsive gambling is a neurotic disease, one of the worst, in that it may mean financial ruin for the victim. As a part of the picture, most habitual gamblers have an unconscious need to lose, though this is never consciously recognized and would be denied. Unconsciously, mistakes will be made to insure loss. Any run of luck is quickly followed by further play and eventual loss.

One of my patients was an illegal bookmaker with a beautiful wife and two fine children. He worked for a syndicate and was "small fry" himself but made better than a thousand a week on an average. All went back into his own bets on the races. Of course he continually lost. His family even went hungry sometimes. He visited me because of insomnia over his worries. But he did not want to quit gambling. His wife pleaded with him to stop, without result. I was unable to persuade him that he needed treatment for a neurotic compulsion. He was sure he would win next time. I saw him only once and shortly afterward read of his suicide. His wife told me he had "borrowed" a large sum of money which he had collected for the syndicate and had lost it betting. No doubt he feared reprisals. In this gambling compulsion there is usually a strong need for self-punishment. That is why the victim unconsciously wishes to lose.

If you are a frequent gambler and lose most of the time you might question your subconscious and discover whether or not you fall into the compulsive gambler category. Then you should try to find out the sources of any guilt feelings which are calling for self-punishment. If self-hypnosis and autosuggestion fail to help you overcome this, you would be wise to visit a psychologist or psychiatrist for help. As this condition is a definite neurosis, self-help may not be successful.

**How to set goals for yourself.** I continually find among my patients a lack of any definite goals. Presumably this must be true of many people, for only a small percentage meet with great success in life. Of course many others are moderately successful and reasonably happy. To be happy and contented it is essential to have definite goals. Even reaching toward them and partially fulfilling them is rewarding.

Among the causes for this situation can be found plain, everyday laziness and a lack of ambition. The fear-producing emotions are often also a part of the picture. Fear of failure is common. If one doesn't try, he can't fail and so this fear is quieted. Expectation of something disastrous makes a goal seem not worthwhile. Negative thinking makes it seem impossible to reach a goal, so why waste the effort? Lack of confidence and feelings of inferiority add to the motives for failure to set goals.

If minor aims are set and realized, it becomes easier to reach more important ones. Doing well with some form of hobby can be a first step. However, there should be a real interest in the hobby, and it should be along some line where a talent or ability can be utilized.

A more important goal could be the determination to work well so that an increase in wages or salary and in position will follow. Positive thinking, determination and effort will pay off within a reasonable time. Then a further goal along the same line should be set. If there is dissatisfaction with the type of work you do, set a goal of obtaining another job, perhaps in some different field. If you do not like your work, success and happiness are not likely to be found.

What goals should you have? Essentially the main one is happiness, with health included. All others involve striving for this. Financial security is a most important one. A satisfactory marriage and family life would probably be near the head of the list. Certainly good health is another vitally important aim. Success in your occupation, other than in its financial aspect, should be included. Less important than these are social recognition, being liked and approved, these satisfying the herd instinct. In reaching these goals there should also be included that of knowing yourself, for it is the key to success with the others.

**Overcoming inferiority and poverty complexes.** The first step in removing your inferiority feelings is to make a complete reassessment of yourself. Write out just what you think of yourself, including as well as possible why you have such opinions. Writing them out is better than merely thinking them over as you tend to think more clearly about the problem when you write. No one need see what you have written and it can be thrown away or destroyed afterwards.

What are the things in childhood which led you to form the image you now hold of yourself? Were you rejected by your parents? Did they belittle you and scold or punish you for your failures? Did they overprotect you? What about your relationship to sisters and brothers, particularly those older than you? Did you feel you could not compete with them? All these are some of the sources of inferiority feelings.

Next you should make a personal inventory of yourself in the form of a statement of assets and liabilities, such as an accountant would make for a business firm. Such a listing is given here so you will not overlook important points. On it you can check yourself against all these factors. You may be able to think of others fitting your own individuality. If you are interested enough in helping yourself to be reading this book, it is almost a certainty that your assets far outweigh your liabilities.

It is impossible for you to assess yourself correctly in every detail. Ask someone, or more than one, in your family who knows you well to do the same summing up. You will find that they hold a very different view about you on some things, and probably a much more correct one.

The purpose of this exercise is to help you take a better and more realistic viewpoint of yourself—changing your self-image to a more correct one. You have undoubtedly been exaggerating your weaknesses and overlooking many of your assets. Your poor opinion of yourself in some ways is undoubtedly overstretched and you have been seeing yourself through the wrong end of the telescope. In reviewing the list, see the errors in your total assessment.

Autosuggestion can help in changing your views. Give your subconscious some prodding so its ideas also will change. Tell it you are a pretty good sort after all, with lots of good points and abilities, and that in the future you will be correcting some of the liabilities.

More self-help can be carried out by reviewing things in your childhood which have led to your mistaken viewpoints. Questioning with the pendulum or finger responses can help locate these experiences. Work also along this line to locate reasons for guilt feelings—seeking the things in your past where you feel you have done wrong. Have not most of them been quite minor? Should you perhaps feel now so guilty about them? Should you not perhaps feel that you have made mistakes, but have learned from them and will not repeat them? Then they can be water under the bridge.

Salter in his book *Conditioned Reflex Therapy* (Farrar, Straus & Cudahy, New York), has recommended some good exercises aimed at overcoming inferiority ideas. Practicing these will gradually act to build up your ego. (1) *Say what you feel,* uttering aloud any spontaneously felt emotion. If you are angry say so in an acceptable way. If your feelings are hurt do not withdraw but express the hurt. Apply this idea to any emotion experienced. (2) *Contradict and attack.* When you disagree with someone about some matter, say so instead of remaining silent or agreeing. It can be done politely. State your own ideas. (3) *Use the word 'I' frequently and with emphasis.* "I think this." Capitalize the *I* emphasizing it by saying it louder. (4) *When anyone praises you for anything, agree with them* instead of deprecating yourself with some phrase like "oh, it's nothing." Admit you did well. (5) *Improvise and live more for the moment.* Do not plan ahead to any extent.

Salter calls this a developing of "excitory conditioned reflexes" to counteract inhibitory ones. He recommends much aggressiveness in practicing these points. This is needed, but in my opinion this can be overdone and better results will come if you are positive but not too aggressive. Being very positive is important, great aggressiveness will bring results too but will be harder for the inhibited person to show. Also, if overdone it would probably bring resentment and dislike from others, which is not to be desired. All these points can be practiced and carried out in an acceptable way. They will be found very valuable in helping to overcome inadequacy feelings.

One of the end products of this feeling of inferiority is insecurity, which is a fear. Another is fear of failure. Still others are characteristics such as shyness, lack of aggressiveness, sensitivity, indecisiveness, dependency, a tendency to withdraw. All add up to immaturity and fear.

Correcting your wrong impressions about yourself and revising your visual image overcomes negativism and changes your disabling character traits so that your subconscious mind can guide you to success and happiness. The brakes you have been applying are removed. The two basic goals of the subconscious are the pursuit of pleasure and happiness and the avoidance of pain. Self-appreciation and a proper viewpoint of yourself is a long step towards both.

**Your balance sheet or self-inventory.** When you are checking and scoring the following balance sheet of your assets and liabilities, use a pencil so you can erase the scoring. Make a note of the results. Then with the pendulum ask questions of your subconscious about each item and again add up your score. You probably will be surprised to find the subconscious disagreeing on some parts of the inventory. You can ask such question as, "Am I really lazy?" "And am I really decisive?" "Am I really stupid?" "Am I actually disliked?" You should find it quite interesting to learn what your subconscious thinks about some of these attributes. This may help you to change some of your ideas about yourself.

If possible you should also ask others who are close to you and know you well to score you. You probably will find their opinions differing in some respects from your own. Again, this should help you in your revision of ideas.

When you have completed your scoring, review your liabilities and decide which ones can be most easily changed. Merely being more aware of them will make it possible for you to start changing some of them. Some

can be altered readily with a little effort; others will take
more work and you will have to force yourself. Self-suggestion can help to correct some of them.

About a year after you have completed your self-help
program you might score yourself again. This allows plenty
of time for changes which undoubtedly will continue at a
subconscious level after you complete your program. Your
score will be quite different from the original one.

## SUMMARY

In carrying out your program it is of the utmost importance for you to take a proper viewpoint of yourself.
If you have physical disabilities or deformities of any
kind do not exaggerate their importance, for you can
rise above them. Probably you have many qualities and
abilities which greatly outweigh them.

If you have strong feelings of unworthiness, of inferiority and insecurity, some introspection and review
of your childhood should lead you to their sources. Review the attitude and behavior of your parents toward
you.

Consider your situation as to goals. They are very
important. You may have some but perhaps you need to
set up further goals. Good health and happiness depend
on feelings of security, a good family life, and social
recognition. With good health added, you should be
relatively happy. With goals to work toward your health
will be good, both physical and mental health.

To overcome inferiority feelings you should reassess
yourself. Your attitudes toward yourself can be changed
by seeing how they developed during childhood, by
autosuggestion, by using Salter's exercises, and by investigating any sources of guilt in order to remove any need
for self-punishment. Reassessment is best made by appraising yourself with the balance sheet which follows,
preferably having others close to you also score you
with it.

## BALANCE SHEET OF CHARACTER, PHYSICAL AND OTHER ATTRIBUTES

Some of the traits listed here are of more importance than others. Each one is followed by three numbers giving its value, some lower, some higher. In scoring yourself, estimate this value. For instance, with the trait *decisive,* if you are inclined to hesitate but reach decisions fairly well, you should score three points. If you believe you are able to decide well, score 4 points; if very decisive, score 5. Under *finances,* if yours are fair, score 3 points, 4 if good, 5 if excellent. For *education,* if you have finished high school score 3; if a college graduate, score 4; post-graduate degree, score 5.

In the liability column, take *irritable* as an example. If somewhat irritable, score 2; often irritable score 3; very irritable score 4. For *appearance,* if you believe you are not very good looking, score 3; if homely score 4; and if definitely ugly, score 5. If you feel that you cannot judge yourself about any attitude, leave the score blank.

Place your score in the square before each trait. When you have checked all, add the scores for assets and the scores for liabilities. Then compare the totals and you will have a good "bird's-eye" view of your qualities. If you have someone else who is close to you also score you, this will give you a much better perspective of yourself.

### ASSETS

#### Character Traits

☐ Are you honest?  3, 4, 5.
☐ Are you ambitious?  3, 4, 5.
☐ Are you kind?  3, 4, 5.
☐ Are you thoughtful of others?  3, 4, 5.
☐ Are you truthful?  3, 4, 5.
☐ Are you positive?  3, 4, 5.
☐ Are you efficient?  3, 4, 5.
☐ Are you decisive?  3, 4, 5.
☐ Are you energetic?  3, 4, 5.
☐ Are you courageous?  3, 4, 5.
☐ Are you constructively aggressive?  3, 4, 5.
☐ Are you good-humored?  3, 4, 5.
☐ Do you face reality and problems?  3, 4, 5.
☐ Are you sincere?  2, 3, 4.
☐ Are you patient?  2, 3, 4.
☐ Are you tolerant?  2, 3, 4.
☐ Are you generous?  2, 3, 4.

ASSETS *(cont.)*

- ☐ Are you open to conviction? 2, 3, 4.
- ☐ Can you concentrate well? 2, 3, 4.
- ☐ Are you punctual? 1, 2, 3.

### Physical Attributes

- ☐ Do you have good health? 3, 4, 5.
- ☐ Is your appearance fair, good, or handsome (or beautiful)? 3, 4, 5.
- ☐ Is your general build good, very good, excellent? 3, 4, 5.
- ☐ Are you well-coordinated, skillful? 3, 4, 5.
- ☐ Do you have good stature? 1, 2, 3.
- ☐ Do you have good vision? 2, 3, 4.

### Miscellaneous Attributes

- ☐ Do you have good intelligence? 3, 4, 5.
- ☐ Do you have goals? 3, 4, 5.
- ☐ Do you have talents? 3, 4, 5.
- ☐ Do you have a good education? 3, 4, 5.
- ☐ Do you have a good job? 3, 4, 5.
- ☐ Are your finances good? 3, 4, 5.
- ☐ Do you have a good marriage? 3, 4, 5.
- ☐ Do you have children? Score 5 for each.
- ☐ Do you have social recognition? 2, 3, 4.
- ☐ Are you well liked? 3, 4, 5.
- ☐ Do you have good ability at sports or athletics? 2, 3, 4.

_____

_____

_____

LIABILITIES

### Character Traits

- ☐ Are you dishonest? 3, 4, 5.
- ☐ Are you untrustworthy? 3, 4, 5.
- ☐ Are you inefficient? 3, 4, 5.
- ☐ Are you unkind, cruel, sadistic? 3, 4, 5.
- ☐ Are you self-centered, egoistic? 3, 4, 5.
- ☐ Are you depressed? 3, 4, 5.

LIABILITIES (*cont.*)

- [ ] Are you negative? 3, 4, 5.
- [ ] Do you have anxiety? 3, 4, 5.
- [ ] Do you have guilt feelings? 3, 4, 5.
- [ ] Do you have inferiority feelings? 3, 4, 5.
- [ ] Do you escape from responsibilities? 3, 4, 5.
- [ ] Are you fearful, phobic? 3, 4, 5.
- [ ] Are you indecisive? 3, 4, 5.
- [ ] Are you lazy? 2, 3, 4.
- [ ] Are you selfish? 2, 3, 4.
- [ ] Are you irritable? 2, 3, 4.
- [ ] Are you indifferent? 1, 2, 3.
- [ ] Are you critical? 1, 2, 3.
- [ ] Are you impatient? 1, 2, 3.
- [ ] Do you have difficulty concentrating? 1, 2, 3.
- [ ] Are you a perfectionist? 1, 2, 3.
- [ ] Are you opinionated? 1, 2, 3.
- [ ] Are you a worrier? 1, 2, 3.
- [ ] Are you too aggressive? 1, 2, 3.
- [ ] Are you too passive? 1, 2, 3.

*Physical Attributes*

- [ ] Do you have poor health? 3, 4, 5.
- [ ] Is your appearance poor, homely, ugly? 3, 4, 5.
- [ ] Is your build poor, quite poor, very poor? 3, 4, 5.
- [ ] Is your stature short? 2, 3, 4.
- [ ] Are you awkward? 1, 2, 3.
- [ ] Do you have poor vision? 1, 2, 3.

*Miscellaneous Attributes*

- [ ] Do you have a poor education? 3, 4, 5.
- [ ] Are your finances poor? 3, 4, 5.
- [ ] Are you stupid? 3, 4, 5.
- [ ] Do you have a poor marriage? 3, 4, 5.
- [ ] Are you disliked? 2, 3, 4.
- [ ] Do you have a poor memory? 2, 3, 4.
- [ ] Are you dissatisfied with your job? 2, 3, 4.
- [ ] Do you drink too much? 3, 4, 5.

- [ ] Total score for Assets
- [ ] Total score for Liabilities

# Chapter 10

# HOW TO CONQUER BAD
# HABITS AND OVERCOME PAIN

Before we take up the main part of your program of self-treatment, this chapter will be of value to you if you ever are n pain for any reason. And if you are a smoker and wish to quit, some of the ideas about ending that habit will be helpful.

**Do you want to stop smoking?** Some of the books dealing with hypnosis have reported its use as a means of stopping smoking. Unfortunately, the impression has been given that all one needs to do is to be hypnotized and told one will no longer desire to smoke and he is then instantly freed of the habit. There have been some who have found this true—about one in a hundred. In isolated instances it *has* worked almost like magic.

For the cigarette addict to stop is no easy matter, even with the help of hypnosis, and hypnosis can indeed be a help. Most who try to stop smoking have great difficulty and go through a period of much discomfort. I have heard a number of ex-smokers tell of their success in stopping by their own efforts, and how this was accomplished. I have helped a number of others to stop with hypnosis. There have also been failures with still others who were not able to break the habit.

When one makes a definite decision to quit smoking and determines that he will do so, I do not believe he needs any help in carrying out his project. He will stop and does not find it too difficult. Those who end the habit in this way often comment on having been surprised at how easy it was to stop.

Most people who try to stop have decided they should do so because it is a dirty, expensive habit and a menace to health. Believing that they should and wanting to stop are not the same thing. They do not want to stop; they want to continue and to satisfy their oral need. They wish to stop on an intellectual basis, but have not made up their minds to do so. Wishful thinking is mixed with negative thoughts. It is going to be so hard to do it. It will be a long, miserable time before the craving is done. Such a person strongly doubts his ability to stop. Then, when he tries, our old acquaintance, the law of reversed effect, steps in and he fails.

**A successful approach to the problem.** There seems to be only one successful approach to this problem. That is to make up your mind firmly that you not only are going to be an ex-smoker but also that you *can* do it without the shadow of a doubt. You are stronger than an infernal weed. You are no longer going to be its slave and the time has now come when you will no longer smoke.

With this determination some will find it easy to stick to the resolution. Others will have more difficulty but will break the habit. Autosuggestion under hypnosis can ease the process. This should include impressing the subconscious with the reasons for stopping. Positive suggestions to minimize desire should be made. It is a mistake to suggest no desire at all for there is bound to be some craving.

In planning when to cut off, it is better to set it two days in the future and then to smoke about twice your usual number of cigarettes for those two days. By their end, you will be fed up and cigarettes will taste so bad that you are glad to stop.

A few people find they can cut down the number smoked, using fewer each day and then none at all. With most this is unsuccessful. You either smoke or you don't smoke. There are several things which will help one over the first few days of withdrawal. An oral need is involved in smoking and other means of satisfying it can be resorted to. Life Savers or fruit drops can be sucked as a substitute or gum can be chewed. Drugstores sell an imitation cigarette which can be used as an alternative, or a piece of wooden doweling the size of a cigarette will do. There are drugs requiring no prescription which offer some help. These tend to counteract the actual nicotine craving which

persists for a time. It has been said that all nicotine will
not be out of your system until about six days after
stopping.

**How to control desire.** Some who stop report feeling
very irritable for a time. This would seem to arise from
resentment at having to go through the unpleasant experience of stopping. There is often a tendency to add some
weight, for the taste buds begin to function better when
you no longer smoke and food is much more tasty. The
oral need may also cause you to eat more. Suggestion
should be effective in counteracting these tendencies.

When the desire for a cigarette is felt, it should be
counteracted immediately with the thought, "I no longer
smoke and I don't need to," followed by diverting the
mind to something else.

When the addiction is broken, the thought of smoking
seldom enters the mind. However there seem to be two
danger periods at which time you may find yourself smoking again. About three months after quitting there is a
strong chance you will wonder what a cigarette would
now taste like. If you take one to find out, you probably
will be a smoker again. This same thought seems to in-
trude about a year after you have quit. With forewarning
of the likelihood of having such thoughts and awareness
of the danger, it can be avoided. The situation is something like that of the alcoholic—there is one drink between him and the gutter. There is one cigarette between
you and being a smoker again.

There are statistics as to the longevity of smokers and
non-smokers. The more you smoke, the shorter your life,
perhaps by as much as ten years, according to the figures.
It has been shown that lung cancer occurs far more frequently, ten to one, with smokers than with non-smokers.
The British government has taken official notice of this
fact and has staged a publicity campaign, urging its citizens
to abstain. The sale of cigarettes in that country has since
declined dramatically, which shows that many can stop
smoking. Approaching the problem as outlined above will
enable you to whip the habit, that your days on earth
be longer.

**How you can control pain.** Not everyone can learn to
control pain, but it can be done if a medium state of
autohypnosis can be reached. Since many readers will
learn self-hypnosis well enough to produce anesthesia,
they should know how to do it.

There are other ways of controlling pain, to some extent, besides hypnotic anesthesia, or drugs. The pain threshold is automatically raised when you are well relaxed. You may still feel pain, but to a lesser degree. Every dentist knows this and tries to have his patient relax as much as possible if the dental session is to be painful in any way. The patient probably enters the dental office fearful and tense. His tension has lowered the pain threshold. One of the main uses of hypnosis in dentistry is to relax the patient so he will feel less pain. He probably will not even feel the insertion of a hypodermic needle.

Another way to control pain is by distraction of attention. Have you ever had the experience of suddenly noticing that you are bleeding, perhaps rather profusely? Hunting the source of the blood, you find you have cut yourself but were not aware of how or when you did it. Your attention was distracted and so pain wasn't felt. The moment you discovered the blood and then its source, you began to feel the pain. In battle, soldiers sometimes are wounded but for a time are unaware of it. In the excitement, with their attention distracted, they do not feel the impact of a bullet or shell fragment and are not aware of the wound. When awareness comes, pain begins.

A LESSON IN PSYCHOLOGY FROM A VETERINARY. My daughter once owned a kitten which I took to a veterinary for enteritis shots, two of which are given a week apart. The assistant took the kitten at the first visit. He placed it on a table and reached for the hypodermic syringe. The animal sensed something unpleasant was about to happen and began struggling and yowling. The assistant asked me to help hold it. I grasped its legs while he held its head with one hand and inserted the needle in its back with the other. As he gave the injection the kitten wailed loudly from the pain.

Next week when I came the older veterinary took it. As he placed it on the table I asked if he wanted me to help hold it. "Oh no," he answered, "that's not necessary." Putting his hand behind the kitten's head, he began to bump its nose up and down on the table while he reached for the syringe with the other hand. Deftly inserting the needle, he gave the injection with the kitten not even whimpering. It was too busy wondering what was happening to its nose to feel pain.

**Reliving an experience as a way of modifying pain.** A way of modifying pain can readily be practiced. If you have been hurt—let us say that you have sprained an

ankle—sit or lie down and with your eyes closed review the accident. In your mind's eye go back to the
moment just before the ankle was injured. What were
you doing at the time? What were you looking at? What
actions were you performing, and where were you? Notice
all these things and try to see, to hear, to be aware of
your bodily movements and position as the accident happened. Notice if anything was said by someone. Recapture
your thoughts of the moment. On turning the ankle, what
emotion did you feel? As you do all this, you may feel
the pain increase, for it will have diminished since the
actual injury. Continue through whatever occurred during the next two or three moments after the accident.

After going through this experience, go back to the
start of it and go through it again. Repeat this three or
four times. You will find some of the scene becoming
more vivid but each time there will be much less pain
noticed at the moment you suffered the sprain. When you
have completed this mental exercise, you will find the
ankle much less painful, perhaps only a little sore when
you move it. Incidentally, for some reason this reliving
of the accident will cause the injury to heal much faster.

You might add to this "treatment" by asking your subconscious a few questions with pendulum or finger responses. Was there some subconscious reason why you
turned your ankle? If the answer is yes, try to uncover
whatever motivation was involved. The injury may have
been entirely accidental, without motivation, or there may
have been some reason behind it.

**How you can induce hypnotic anesthesia.** While you
are in autohypnosis, anesthesia can be induced in several
ways. Two of the best methods will be given here. The
deeper you are in hypnosis the better the results will be.

When pain is stimulated, the pain nerves work through
electric impulses which travel along the nerve channels
and are registered in the brain. These are even measurable
with an instrument called a myograph. In theory, a local
anesthetic drug such as novocaine paralyzes or blocks the
nerves so the electric current does not reach the brain.
Then no pain is felt.

The same thing presumably happens with hypnotic
anesthesia. While in hypnosis, with your eyes closed, imagine you have in your head a long row of electric light
switches and visualize a little electric light above each
switch. Each light is a different color or shade of color
and all are turned on. There is a switch with a red light

above it, one with a pink light, a dark blue one, a light blue, an orange, etc., with all colors and many shades. Each switch goes to a different part of your body.

You are now going to produce anesthesia in one hand, whichever you select for the purpose. The switch with the light blue light goes to the hand you have chosen. Now imagine you are turning off that switch and see the light blue light go out.

For it to be anesthetized it is not necessary for you to feel a numbness in the hand, but you may or may not have this sensation. If you have ever experienced novocaine at your dentist's, you might aim to develop numbness just as you felt it before. You can suggest, repeating it three or four times, "My hand is becoming slightly numb and will get more and more numb. It may have a feeling of coldness in it." Add to this suggestion, "I am going to pinch my hand in a moment and it will be completely anesthetized. At first I will pinch lightly and each time I pinch the anesthesia will increase. When I have pinched four times the anesthesia will be complete."

When you feel the numbness wait for it to increase a little, then start pinching various places on your hand, increasing the strength of the pinch a little each time. Then pinch with your fingernails as hard as you can. In doing this you will feel pressure, and be aware of pinching, but there will be no pain. It will not hurt. It will be as though you are pinching a thin leather glove.

The first time you practice this, you may find your hand is not completely anesthetized. The anesthesia may be only partial. But for a comparison, pinch the other hand as hard as you pinched the anesthetized one. You will almost certainly notice a great difference.

Success will depend somewhat on the depth of hypnosis and on your mental attitude. Doubts in your mind will impede and the anesthesia may be only partial. Skepticism acts to prevent your suggestions from being completely accepted by the subconscious and all the pain nerves are not shut off. The subconscious can close the nerve currents just as an anesthetic drug paralyzes the nerves.

Skepticism can be counteracted by a realization of how thoroughly anesthesia through hypnosis can be developed. Thousands of women in this country have been able to go through childbirth with it. Dr. Ralph August, of Muskegon, Michigan, has written a book on this subject, telling of over a thousand cases of his own where delivery was with hypnotic anesthesia.

In some of these cases some pain was felt by the woman, but it was greatly modified. About half had no pain at all. A number of anesthesiologists now use hypnosis at times and many cases of major surgery have been performed with no drugs of any kind used. It has been used for leg amputations, for cardiac operations, for lung resections, and in many other conditions of major surgery. Of course the usual procedure is with drugs, but sometimes conditions prevent their use. The knowledge that hypnotic anesthesia can be so complete will better help you to develop it.

If you become a very good subject in autohypnosis, a simpler technique will serve. With this you merely suggest anesthesia in the hand. Phrase it something like this. "My right hand will become completely anesthetized when I have stroked it three times with my left hand. I will feel pressure but it will not hurt when I pinch it." Continue with the suggestion of increased anesthesia with each pinch. Then test as with the former method.

When you have learned to shut off pain in a hand, you will be able to do it in any other part of the body, using the same method. Probably the greatest use you will have will be when you visit your dentist. Ask him to give you a moment or two to put yourself into hypnosis and to produce anesthesia. You can then set it up in either or both jaws and have your dental work done in comfort. The dentist may wish to use novocaine as well. If you have become proficient, this is unnecessary.

Always remember to remove the anesthesia. You can retain it for several days if you wish, restoring it if it is lost overnight. This might be desirable if dental work is performed where there would be pain for several days, as with tooth extraction. But be sure to end the anesthesia when it has served its purpose. Pain is intended to make us aware of injury or of something wrong at the seat of pain. There is no reason to continue to feel it when the purpose is served.

**Sometimes pain has a psychological cause.** Physicians sometimes are visited by a patient who complains of a pain someplace in the body, perhaps in a limb, but more often in the chest or abdominal area. No reason for it is found and after many tests the doctor is unable to make a diagnosis. Both patient and doctor are puzzled and frustrated. The patient will be certain there is some physical reason for the pain, which may be quite severe at times. In this situation an exploratory operation may be

decided on. Many an abdomen has been opened and
nothing found which could be causing the pain. Before
operating the physician who is oriented toward psychological causes would investigate this aspect. Such a pain
can hurt as much as any organic one. It is not all in the
patient's head—the pain is real.

While attending one of our symposiums, a physician
asked to be a demonstration subject as he was suffering
from a pain, severe at times, located in his back below
the right shoulder blade. He believed the pain could be
controlled by means of hypnotic anesthesia. About a
month before the meeting the doctor had experienced a
coronary attack. He was recovering but had not returned
to work and was impatient to resume his practice. He
described the shoulder pain as being definitely organic.

The instructor who was demonstrating questioned Dr.
P. with pendulum responses. The first question was as to
whether there was any psychological cause for the pain.
The pendulum moved to say *yes,* to the surprise of the
physician who replied verbally before the pendulum
moved, saying, "The answer to that is no." His subconscious mind did not seem to agree! Futher questioning
followed.

Q. Is it all right for you to know what psychological factors
are precipitating this pain?
A. *Yes* (pendulum).*
Q. Is it all right for me and the audience to know this?
A. *Yes.*
Q. Is self-punishment involved?
A. *No.*
Q. Has someone ever said anything to you that might be
resulting in the pain? Is there some suggestion working?
A. *No.*
Q. Is the pain associated in some way to a past experience
of any kind?
A. *Yes.*
Q. Was it something that occurred before you were twenty
years old?
A. *Yes.*
Q. Did it happen before you were ten years old?
A. *Yes.*
Q. Was it before you were five?
A. *Yes.*
Q. Before two?
A. *Yes.*

* Pendulum and finger responses are in italics.

Q. Before you were one year old?

A. *No.*

Q. Was it concerned with an illness?

A. *No.*

Q. With an accident?

A. *Yes.*

Q. Did it happen indoors rather than outdoors?

A. *No.*

Q. Was any other person involved?

A. *I don't know.* (Later it was seen that this question could not be answered correctly. There was another person present but she witnessed it rather than being actually involved.)

Q. Were you hurt at the time?

A. *Yes.*

Q. Was it your right shoulder that was hurt?

A. *Yes.*

As the questions were being asked and Dr. P. concentrated on the lucite ball, he had slipped spontaneously into hypnosis. This was now deepened and with finger responses he was asked if it was all right for him to return to the childhood incident. The answer was *yes.* He was regressed and asked to relate what was happening.

The doctor said he was outdoors, lying in a baby buggy. Asked how old he was, he said it was just after his first birthday. No one was visible to him, but the buggy was rolling down a sidewalk. Then he felt it tip over and he was thrown out on his right shoulder. Finger responses were then made to further questions.

Q. Does this accident have something to do with the present pain?

A. *Yes.*

Q. There is some reason for this. A thought will now come to you as to what the association is.

A. (Verbally) It's my mother.

Q. Does she have something to do with the restimulation of this pain?

A. *Yes.*

Q. Did she do something or say something that caused this?

A. *Yes.* (Then verbally) She said something about a bottle. I don't see the connection though. She was at my home a couple of weeks ago and we had an argument. The pain began that night.

Q. Is there any other cause for the pain?

A. *Yes.*

With more questioning it was established that the pain was serving to keep him from practicing, so he should not return to his office so soon after his coronary attack. His subconscious agreed to modify the pain but it would continue until his recovery was sufficient for him to return safely to his office.

A letter from Dr. P. received two weeks later reported the pain as still present but less intense. His mother remembered the baby buggy incident and had felt very guilty because of her carelessness. The buggy had rolled away from her down a slight hill and had tipped over, throwing him out just as he had described. She was surprised to know he had recalled the experience. It had happened, as he said, a short time after his first birthday. The mother was sure she had never told him about the accident as she had felt so guilty about it.

This case is remarkable because of the recall of such an early memory, and also because Dr. P. was so sure the pain was physically caused. It shows that very early memories are accessible under hypnosis and that the subconscious is aware of the sources of our difficulties.

## SUMMARY

If you wish to stop smoking you can do so with no great difficulty only if you want to quit and are determined to overcome the habit. It is essential to make up your mind that you really wish to quit and be very determined that you can and will do so.

Autosuggestion with self-hypnosis can be of great aid in minimizing the desire and in bolstering your determination. You will need a substitute to satisfy the oral craving that is a part of the smoking habit. Fruit or peppermint drops, chewing gum, or an imitation cigarette can be used. Drugs which will help counteract the nicotine in your system are available at every drugstore.

You must immediately overcome the desire for a cigarette as soon as such a thought pops into your mind. Tell yourself at once that you really don't have to smoke and then divert your mind to something else. If you nurse the thought, you probably will take a cigarette. At times review all the good reasons and motives which have led you to stop smoking.

You have read here how pain can be modified or even eliminated by means of hypnosis. Thousands of women have escaped or greatly modified the pain of childbirth, and many more people have been able to have dental work performed without discomfort.

Practice turning off pain while in self-hypnosis with the use of the imaginary "switches," but don't forget to remove hypnotic anesthesia at the proper time.

Pain can develop from psychological as well as physical causes. It hurts just as much when psychologically caused. Ideomotor replies to questions can show you if pain has a psychological cause. By further questioning you can learn the reasons for it.

# HEAL YOUR OWN
# EMOTIONAL SCARS

It is possible to consider here only some of the more common ailments, or this book would run into several volumes. Basically, self-therapy would be much the same for all.

For many conditions there certainly should be medical treatment. If the situation permits, a psychotherapist should be seen. If none is available or if finances do not allow, self-therapy can be very helpful and successful, but common sense must always be used with it. Another situation where it can be adopted would be where psychotherapy has been a failure or incomplete for some reason. Sometimes much can be accomplished in speeding up the process by occasional visits to a psychotherapist with whom there can be consultation about your progress and results.

In general it is not known why one person under stress or in emotional difficulties will develop stomach ulcers, another will suffer from arthritis, while still another has an allergy. Certain types of people do tend to have ulcers and migraine, for instance, but typing applies only to a few psychosomatic ailments.

**An illness may be a defense.** If you are beginning self-treatment, approach it with hope and the expectation of getting well. However, this is only a conscious attitude. Perhaps your inner mind has a different view, which must be considered as possible. Most of our emotional troubles,

133

including psychosomatic illness, are defense mechanisms. The subconscious is trying to solve a problem in the best way it can; the method it chooses may not be very good, perhaps it may even be detrimental. The subconscious is not logical in its thinking, nor does it look at end results. If something is serving as a defense and is aimed at preserving you, the inner mind does not want to lose its defense, to have its applecart upset.

This being true, self-therapy may seem to the subconscious to be a threat to its defenses. Resistance is then stimulated and the going may be rough. The goal must be clearly defined so your subconscious understands it. You are not intending to rob yourself of defenses. Through an understanding of causes, through insight into the reasons for a condition you intend to make the symptom or condition unnecessary. With insight, both your conscious and subconscious viewpoints should change and what was needed as a defense becomes superfluous. The need is gone. Best results come when the inner mind is cooperative and carries out your suggestions, instead of resisting them.

Resistance may very well provoke thoughts and rationalizations which the subconscious will push into your conscious mind intended to cause you to stop "monkeying" with its defenses. These will be negative thoughts. "This self-treatment is going to take a long time (not necessarily true). I probably will get nowhere with it, and why try? I'll just pass it up." Sometimes you may be making excellent progress and are approaching something traumatic and repressed. You may find yourself making all sorts of excuses to postpone further self-treatment. A fixed idea in the subconscious can have the same effect as repression. When such an idea is operating, nothing can be accomplished until it is removed. Such phrases as "Nothing does any good." "What's the use?" "You'll never get anywhere," "You must learn to live with it," "You'll never get over it," and still others conveying similar ideas are able to stop progress and block results until removed.

If suspected as present, anything of this nature can be located by questioning of the subconscious. Such phrases have origins somewhere in your past life. The idea, which is exactly like a posthypnotic suggestion in operation, can then be eliminated so it will have no further effect.

When these phrases are working they are likely to be spoken and repeated from time to time. This is also true of phrases found in organ language, such as "It's a head-ache to me." When you notice yourself uttering such phrases, check to see if they may be affecting your behavior.

**Safeguards in your self-therapy.** Two precautions are important in self-therapy and should be observed. Your subconscious has knowledge as to the causes of conditions. You wish to learn about them. It also has all the data you have ever learned stored away in your memory. This part of the mind always works to protect you. Sometimes the past experience which may be concerned in producing some symptom may be so horrible that is deeply buried and would be intolerable if you suddenly remembered it. This is seldom so, but it is a possibility. It could be dangerous to try to reach it. In all probability, your subconscious would protect you by keeping it unavailable to the conscious mind, but you can check as to any danger by ideomotor responses to questions. When you are about to delve into the reasons for any symptom or condition, ask the question, "Is it all right for me to know the causes of this?" If the answer is *yes,* there is perfect safety. If *no,* narrow the question down. "Is there some factor I am not ready to know but others I could know?" With several things pertaining, it might be quite all right to know everything but one and you could proceed.

The other safety device is similar. Take the precaution of questioning your subconscious before ever trying to regress yourself to some past experience. "Is it all right for me to go back and recall this experience?" If it is too overwhelming or threatening it would probably be impossible to reach the event, but this safety factor will protect you from any possible danger.

Having read this far, you have learned some of the techniques you will use in your self-treatment. You should practice the preliminaries before setting to work. You should learn to relax well. You will certainly make better and faster progress if you learn autohypnosis, though it is not essential if you prefer to forego it. You should now understand the way you will deal with autosuggestion, and the means of making it most effective. You have learned how emotional difficulties affect us and the seven main factors for which to look as causative of psychosomatic illnesses and other conditions. These are your seven keys to successful results. Before beginning your self-treatment review the chapters on suggestion and on causes.

**Reviewing the seven elements commonly causing emo-**

**tional ailments.** For convenience it may be well to state
again these seven elements: (1) conflicts, (2) motivations, (3) effect of suggestion, (4) organ language, (5)
identification, (6) self-punishment, and (7) past experiences. These are the sources you will be investigating. You
will try to learn which apply and which are not involved,
eliminating those not concerned. Any or all may enter the
picture.

You will ask questions of your subconscious aimed at
finding out the ones involved. "Is there some motivation
for this condition?" (Specify the condition or symptom.)
When you have an affirmative answer about any of the
seven factors, you then try to learn more. In this case
you would seek to find what the motivation may be. Some
possible question could be, "Is this motive serving to protect me in some way?" "Is it serving some other purpose?" "Is it getting me out of something?" "Am I seeking sympathy and attention?" "Is it preventing me from
doing something?" From your own knowledge of yourself
you should be able to think of other questions which may
apply.

As to conflict, it may be so superficial that you are already aware of it, or it may be deeply buried. If there is
conflict and you cannot pinpoint it consciously, questioning may locate it and let you learn its nature. There
can be many types of conflict, sex being a frequent source
of trouble.

If suggestions are found to be involved, locate their
nature and when they originated. You can find when they
happened by questions bracketing the years. In the case
histories cited later you will learn more as to how to phrase
questions and the ways to ask them, as well as more about
what to look for. Having found when an incident occurred, learn where, and who may have been present; then
inquire as to what kind of incident. Was it frightening?
Did it have to do with an illness or operation? In query-
ing as to location, was it indoors or outdoors, was it at
home, at school, at a friend's, at a doctor's office. This
same type of questioning would also be used to locate any
kind of past experience, such as a traumatic one.

In inquiring as to identification, the first question should
be, "Am I identifying with someone else as a cause of this
condition—trying to be like someone else?" When affirmative, ask as to whom and try to find why.

When dealing with organ language, ask first, "Is this
symptom some idea which is being carried out by my

subconscious with the physical condition then resulting?" Depending on the symptom, you can be specific. "Do I have this headache because something unpleasant is a headache to me?" would be an example.

If self-punishment is a factor, inquiry can quickly determine the answer. Then your questions should be directed at learning why this is needed and what you feel guilty about. Here past experiences may also be implicated and you should locate them and learn their nature.

Such is the general procedure you will follow in gaining insight into causes. Understanding the reasons is necessary, but there must also be a digestive process following the gaining of knowledge. Conscious understanding is not all, for the views of the subconscious must be changed or modified. It must be led to give up the symptom. Suggestion can be most helpful in bringing this about. Further reviewing of the total situation will also assist in stimulating the digestive process.

In some situations, you must remove the suggestions which are being subconsciously carried out. You must dehypnotize yourself, and there may be conditioned reflexes to be removed. Ways and means will be offered, as you read on, in the discussion of various illnesses and conditions and in the case histories described.

Interpretation of dreams can uncover some of the conflicts and other difficulties which disturb us. Unless the mechanism and symbolism of dreams is known, their meanings may be difficult to understand. To the conscious mind a dream may seem meaningless. The inner mind knows its symbolism and meaning because it produced the dream. In self-therapy it may be possible to interpret a dream without much knowledge of dream mechanisms. While in a trance some people are able to understand the meaning of a dream. The deeper the trance, the more likely this is to be true. When you have had a dream which may seem significant, ask yourself under autohypnosis what it means. You may learn what it signifies.

**How to handle periods of depression.** As has been mentioned, one of the contraindications for self-therapy is when there is great depression. If this is chronic and very strong, the situation is dangerous and something more than self-help is required. Psychiatric help is imperative, for suicide is quite possible. There are more than 25,000 suicides annually, mainly the result of depression.

A study of cycles has shown that everyone has alternating periods of elation and depression with a plateau between. When the degree of these feelings is not great this is normal. The extreme of such a cycle is a condition called a manic-depressive psychosis, a very severe mental illness. With the usual cycle, we feel exceptionally well and mildly elated for about three days, followed by a return to the way we usually feel. Later there comes a three-day period of feeling low and slightly depressed. The length of the cycle is said to vary considerably but to average around 32 to 35 days. Sometimes the peak will be somewhat higher and the depth somewhat lower, which may be a cycle within the cycle.

We are not concerned here with a normal pattern such as this cycle, although one should be aware of it and be cautious of making important decisions either during the elevated period or when at the lower one.

In depression other than the cyclic kind, it is our emotions and confused thinking which are responsible. You cannot be happy when you are depressed, nor depressed when you are happy. They are in direct opposition. When problems are faced and worked out, when fears are overcome, we feel good and depression has vanished.

Dr. Hornell Hart, in another self-help book, *Autoconditioning* (Prentice-Hall, Inc., Englewood Cliffs, New Jersey), stresses our moods and how to control them. He advises making a chart of your moods on a daily basis, listing them from ecstatic at the top, through satisfied and cheerful, and, below a median line, the moods of worried, anxious, discouraged, and so forth down to depressed, with miserable at the very bottom of the list.

Hart's five steps for autoconditioning are first to pick out your problem, next to go off alone and relax using autohypnosis. Then suggestion is applied to overcome the problem. You then awaken yourself and when necessary repeat this, working on the same or different problems. Overcoming your negative and depressed moods will bring happiness and success according to Hart. Undoubtedly this method can be successful with more superficial problems and conflicts.

**Insomnia and how to induce restful sleep.** The sale of sleeping pills in this country runs into the hundreds of millions annually, indicating the great number of people who suffer from insomnia. It is a most unpleasant condition, although no one has ever died from insomnia or even become ill.

Most insomnia stems merely from bad sleeping habits and here self-help should be successful with little difficulty in achieving it. Inability to sleep can be a deep-seated neurotic symptom not easily eliminated. Two types of insomnia are seen. In the one the difficulty is in going to sleep. Sometimes hours pass before the victim drops off. With the other type, sleep comes quickly but the sufferer awakens after three or four hours and cannot get back to sleep. This may be in the middle of the night or along toward morning.

Where insomnia is a bad habit, the person takes his problems and troubles to bed with him, is often a chronic worrier, and his mind is so busy that he does not give himself a chance to fall asleep. The trouble is compounded by negative thoughts and suggestions and by another encounter with the law of reversed effect which we have mentioned so often. He goes to bed, mulls over problems for a while, decides he should try to sleep but from past experience (conditioning) is sure he will not be able to drop off. He tries, putting his thoughts on wanting to sleep and with the law in action becomes wider and wider awake. Finally he becomes so fatigued that he stops trying and promptly falls asleep.

**Fears cause sleeplessness.** Those with a neurotic basis for not sleeping well may fall into either of the insomnia patterns. One of the most common causes is fear, as we have seen in so many other conditions. The insomniac may be afraid to go to sleep. This may be due to a fear of loss of consciousness because then something terrible might happen which could not be controlled.

Another common fear among insomniacs is fear of death. Sleep is associated with death. Such an idea probably originates in childhood. With the difficulty of explaining death to a child when it occurs in the family, it is often said that "Grandma just went to sleep and won't wake up again." Forcing a young child to see a dead person at a funeral, or in the home before the funeral, is a definite trauma. Even worse is to compel the child to kiss the corpse. These things can cause other reactions than insomnia. Those who may have read the book *Three Faces of Eve,* about a case of multiple personality, will remember that being forced as a child to kiss her dead grandmother was a main reason for her personality split. It is incredible that parents would ever force a child into such a frightening and non-understandable situation, but it is sometimes done and is certain to have emotional repercussions.

There are other associations between death and sleep.

Death is often spoken of as "the long sleep." Many children are taught the common little prayer,

> Now I lay me down to sleep,
> I pray the Lord my soul to keep.
> If I should die before I wake,
> I pray the Lord my soul to take.

How does a young child interpret these words? It is a suggestion that he may die during his sleep. The second line also suggests death or that there is danger to the soul while asleep. In uncovering the causes of neurotic insomnia a surprising number of my patients have brought out this prayer as the original source of insomnia, though other factors have also entered. In some of these cases there had been sight of a dead person during childhood, reinforcing the association between sleep and death.

Still other possible reasons for insomnia include the identification with a parent or someone else close in childhood who had insomnia and often talked about it. There may be an element of masochism as a reason, since failure to sleep well is most uncomfortable. Another fear which may prevent sleep comes when one is subject to nightmares. Then he fears to fall asleep because he may have another nightmare.

**Self-therapy uncovers the cause.** With self-therapy all these possibilities must be explored and those which apply must be uncovered and understood. When a fear is consciously recognized and seen as illogical, it may disappear. An adult realizing how the little childhood prayer has affected him will see that death and sleep are not related. It may be necessary to return in memory to the scene in childhood where a dead person was viewed. If the emotions and ideas connected with the experience are worked off, their effect is removed.

Of course, suggestion can also be invoked to aid in sleeping. Other than by removing causes, the best method of ousting insomnia from one's behavior pattern is by means of autohypnosis. I always try to teach insomnia patients to be able to use it. On going to bed and being ready to sleep hypnosis is induced. The suggestion should then be made, "Within a few moments I will be sound asleep and in a deep, refreshing sleep. I will sleep soundly and deeply all night." When this has been done, thoughts should be diverted at once to anything pleasant, avoiding the thought of sleep completely. The phrase "within a

few moments" or the alternative word "soon" is indefinite.
It may be two or three minutes or fifteen or twenty or
more. This allows time for the suggestion to be put into
effect and the subconscious to bring sleep. Continuing to
think about it blocks one, for doubt is apt to enter. The
more certain one can be of accomplishing sleep by this
method, the more sure success will follow.

Since anticipation and fear that one will not go to sleep
play a part, another helpful change of view would be to
tell yourself that lying awake is merely uncomfortable and
annoying and there is no danger involved. "What if I do
lie awake for a while? I can rest, nevertheless. What if it
takes an hour or two before I drop off? So what? I really
do not care. I'll fall asleep after a while." Such thoughts
remove the effect of doubt and anticipation. When you do
not care if you fall asleep now or a bit later, and do not
try, you will slip off very quickly. The law of reversed
effect is thrown out of gear.

Realizing that you do sleep, though not as much or as
well as you would like, and that it does not affect your
health, will remove some of the fear and make it easier
to entertain thoughts like the above.


SHE COULDN'T STAY ASLEEP! One of my patients, Marjorie
we will call her, was a fine example of the person who
has no trouble going to sleep but soon awakens and can't
get back to sleep for a long time. She managed to sleep
several hours each night but much of it was after her
husband rose at six each morning. She slept well until
about nine after this, except on weekends when he did
not go to work.

Marjorie's five or six hours of sleep seemed to be
enough in that she felt well and was in excellent health.
But she complained of how unpleasant it was to lie awake
for hours during the night. Her husband went to bed early,
but she liked to read or watch television until late. She
went to sleep then very promptly but in an hour or two
or a bit more she would awaken and toss the rest of the
night until nearly morning.

She admitted that she found her mind very active at
these times and worried a great deal about problems. In
order to break this habit she was told she must exaggerate
it. Before going to bed each night she was to write out
a list of the things she could worry most about and when
she woke up to take each one and really worry as much

as she could. One of the best ways to break any habit is
to exaggerate it and do it intentionally. After a night or
two of intentional concentrated worrying she found it
harder and harder to do and it began to seem quite
ridiculous.

In order to locate other causes she was questioned with
the pendulum answering:

Q. Is there some other cause or causes for your awakening
during the night?  A. *Yes* (pendulum).

Q. Is there more than one other cause?  A. *Yes.*

Q. Are there more than two other causes?  A. *No.*

Q. Are you punishing yourself by staying awake—is it most
unpleasant for you?  A. *No.*

Q. Is some fear causing you to wake up?  A. *Yes.*

Q. Are you afraid of nightmares—bad dreams?  A. *No.*

Q. Are you afraid you might die during your sleep?  A.
*Yes.*

Q. There is some reason for such a fear. Did you have
some relative die while you were a child and were you told
she had "gone to sleep?"

A. (Verbally) Yes, I remember my Grandmother's funeral.
I was six years old. I was scared when I had to look at her
in her coffin, and they said she was asleep.

Q. Has that childhood experience a bearing on your waking
up?  A. *Yes.*

Q. Is there any other fear working to make you wake up?
A. *No.*

Q. Is there some other motive causing you to awaken?
A. *Yes.*

Q. Is it all right for you to know what it is?  A. *Yes.*

Q. Does it serve some purpose?  A. *Yes.*

Q. Is it connected to some past experience in your life?
A. *No.*

Q. Did one of your parents have insomnia? Are you identifying with someone who had insomnia?  A. *No.*


Several other questions were asked without locating the
other reason for her difficulty. Finally she was told that
when I counted to three a sudden thought would pop
into her mind as to what this other cause could be. She
then said, "Oh, I know. I guess it is to avoid sex. I never
have had any pleasure from it. I guess I'm frigid. I hate
to have my husband approach me and he usually does it
during the night. I guess I wake up so he won't take me
by surprise or so I can be awake and think of some reason to give him to avoid sex."

After a few visits Marjorie was able to lose her frigidity
and following this her insomnia quickly disappeared.

## SUMMARY

Emotionally caused illnesses may be serving as a means of defense. If this is true, you may have such a strong unconscious need for the illness that your inner mind may resist any treatment. But resistance can be overcome and the attitude of the subconscious changed when you uncover the reasons or causes for the illness. Your aim is not to take away a defense but to make it unnecessary.

Questioning your subconscious with ideomotor replies to the questions can uncover the causes. Almost any psychosomatic ailment will be found to have at least one, and probably more, of the seven factors which you have found listed here. These Seven Keys are:

1. Conflict
2. Motivations
3. Effect of suggestion
4. Organ language
5. Identification
6. Self-punishment
7. Past experiences

Learning those that apply as causes for your particular ailment will be a main step toward eliminating it.

You have now read as to how depression sometimes occurs. Mild depression can usually be overcome by learning the reasons for it. If you are very greatly depressed, avoid any self-treatment, for you definitely need psychiatric help.

This chapter will have shown you how you can probably oversome insomnia, if it is one of your troubles, through self-hypnosis. You should inquire with the questioning technique as to the causes. Sometimes insomnia is a very deep-seated neurotic symptom and self-treatment may not be enough to end it. However, most people with this annoying difficulty can end it by learning self-hypnosis, then inducing it when ready to go to sleep and, with a suggestion of dropping off to sleep "within a few moments," will find that the habit can quickly be broken.

*Chapter 12*

# FEARS AND PHOBIAS CAN
# BE CONQUERED

Everyone is subject at times to fears which would not be classed as neurotic and for which there are logical, protective reasons. Anxiety or fear without some definite ground for it is protective, as are phobias, but they are also neurotic symptoms. If you should inquire among your circle of friends and acquaintances you'll find most will admit to some phobia, major or minor.

One of the most common phobias is acrophobia, a dread of high places. Psychology has a long list of scientific terms for various abnormal fears: claustrophobia (fear of confined places), agoraphobia (fear of open spaces), zoophobia (fear of animals), hydrophobia (dread of water). There are many others, these given here being the ones most commonly experienced. A phobia could be defined as a strong, abnormal fear of something.

A phobia is always an unreasonable fear or it could not be classed as a phobia. For instance, there is an almost instinctive dislike of snakes because some snakes are poisonous and dangerous and snakes should therefore be avoided. The garden of Eden story may intensify the distaste for snakes. But if any snake, even one recognized as harmless, causes a panic reaction or a great fear, it is phobic. The matter of degree is important. Even a picture of a snake could then cause panic.

**How phobias develop.** Sometimes a neurotic fear of something is a *displacement*. Something is feared but the thought is so repugnant that the fear is transferred to something else, thus displacing it. It is projected onto the substitute. There is an unreasonable fear of the other object or situation, more often a situation. Such phobias are rare.

More often a phobia is a conditioned reflex set up by some past frightening experience, or a series of similar incidents. These mostly occur in childhood but can come from events in later life. Children in play sometimes will shut a younger child in a dark closet or chest or some other small enclosed place. If left alone in such a place the child will quickly become frightened and perhaps will panic. Near suffocation might happen. It is surprising how often thoughtless parents or relatives will shut a child in a dark closet as a punishment, perhaps leaving him there for some time. Not only claustrophobia but fear of the dark can be generated by such an experience.

Any very frightening experience may lead to a phobia persisting in later life. Near drowning may promote a fear of water. At four years of age my daughter loved to be taken into a swimming pool, though she had not yet learned to swim. One day at the beach, a much older friend led her into shallow water. An unusually large breaker swept her off her feet and rolled her over and over. She swallowed water, choked and became very frightened. Thereafter she cried and refused to go into a pool or to the beach.

Two years later she was old enough to be hypnotized and treated for her phobia. I then regressed her to the beach experience, leading her through it several times, although she cried and objected. But this removed her fears. When she related the story the last time, she even laughed in telling how her friend was also upset by the wave. She quickly learned to swim and to enjoy going in the water again. Without this measure she undoubtedly would have suffered from a fear of water the rest of her life.

**Ridding yourself of a phobia.** In dealing with a phobia by self-treatment, results are usually readily obtained. (This would not be true in the case of a displaced phobia, but these are not at all common.) Uncovering any episode or episodes which fostered the phobia is the main goal. There must also be a discharge of all the emotion tied up with the incident. Merely remembering it is not enough. A psychotherapist would take a patient through the experience again and again. Fear is very strongly felt the first time. Going through it again there is still much emotion but it is less intense. A number of reviews may be needed before all fear is discharged, but each time less is shown. Finally none at all is displayed. Going through the experience three or four times is usually enough, but sometimes more reviews are necessary.

Only by discharging all the emotion is the phobia eliminated. This process is desensitization. Technically, the discharge of the emotion in psychological jargon is called a *catharsis;* reactions to the emotion are called *abreaction.* Events which cause a phobia are excitory. Catharsis by recalling the event is inhibitory.

**Uncovering the frightening event.** In self-therapy it is possible to take oneself back through the frightening event with the use of hypnosis. First, the incident must be located, either from conscious memory of it, or if it has been forgotten and repressed, by the use of ideomotor responses to questions.

Before trying to recall or regress to the event, the question should always be asked, "Is it all right for me to go back through this experience?" The answer rarely would be negative. If it is, you can probably get an affirmative answer at some later time. A negative reply would indicate that the experience was too traumatic to be borne at the moment.

The inhibitory principle can be applied in other situations where fear is present. Dr. Joseph Wolpe has advocated an excellent method of working through fears and phobias and eliminating them in his book *Psychotherapy by Reciprocal Inhibition.**

Dr. Wolpe asks a patient to write out a list of everything which is frightening, disturbing, or embarrassing to him in any way, omitting situations which would frighten anyone, such as being attacked. The patient then is to rewrite the list placing the worst things at the head of the list, and working on down to the least threatening, in order of importance.

**Desensitizing yourself to disturbing situations.** Sessions with the patient then aim to desensitize him to these disturbing situations. Dr. Wolpe teaches him first to relax as much as possible, then the patient is hypnotized, (though this is not essential) and under hypnosis is asked to visualize a scene. The type of scene selected is to be

* Adapted from *Psychotherapy by Reciprocal Inhibition,* by Joseph Wolpe, M.D., with the permission of the publishers, Stanford University Press. © 1958 by the Board of Trustees of Leland Stanford Junior University.

one of the least disturbing situations on the patient's list. It is important to begin at the bottom of the list rather than the top because strong resistance would be encountered then. There will be none over a minor matter.

Several minor disturbing scenes are visualized, taking only a few seconds for each. One of his patients felt minor fear over funerals. He was asked to see a funeral procession from a distance of 200 yards, then to see an empty hearse close up, then a scene at a grave with the coffin taken from the hearse and lowered into the grave. Each scene was repeated several times, and each time the reaction was less. Finally the mild fear about funerals was erased.

In further sessions more disturbing matters are visualized in the same way. Later the seriously upsetting ones are handled and the patient becomes desensitized to all. Reactions to them have become inhibited.

Wolpe states that relaxation during this process is essential and no progress is made without it. There are results without hypnosis but they are much slower. When working through the patient's list, sometimes more situations will be remembered and added to the list.

In self-therapy this technique can be used to overcome fears and phobias. However phobias are best handled by locating their causes and recalling the experience or experiences which generated them, discharging the accompanying emotions. Usually, questioning the subconscious to locate the experience and find its nature is easy. In some of the case histories given later are examples of questioning which will show the type of questions to be asked. If more than one experience is involved, the earliest one in your life should be dealt with first. If one is first located and you have regressed to it and worked off the emotion tied up with it, always ask with the questioning if there is another. Then find it and deal with it.

**How to deal with resistance.** When there is resistance met with and you cannot seem to bring out the incident you are seeking, Wolpe's method may be used, dealing with minor matters. When you have been desensitized to minor fears, you probably will find that you can then reach the experience which has produced the phobia.

A way of temporarily overcoming a fear and eventually ending it is by invoking a stronger emotion when fear is actually being felt. If a person has stage fright or becomes afraid when speaking before a group, he will speak only when he has some motive to do so which is stronger than

the fear. A student called on to recite in class would have
the motivation of passing the course. This probably would
be strong enough to enable him to speak despite his fear.
There would also be the desire to avoid embarrassment.
As he continued to speak, his fear would lessen or disappear after a time. With repetition of such a situation,
the fear would be less each time at the start, and eventually would be ended. But a better method of therapy
would be to learn the reasons behind the fear of speaking
in public.

It should be noted that Wolpe's method is based on the
use of visual imagery. There is also the direct suggestion
that this method will bring results and rid one of his fears.

Phobias mainly develop from past experiences, sometimes from conflicts, and possibly from suggestions where
a child is taught to be afraid of something. If a parent
is phobic about some situation, the child may pick it up
from the parent, partly from identification and partly from
suggestion, in that if the parent is afraid, then the situation is dangerous and the child should be afraid. Always
there is confused, wrong thinking in interpreting the situation and it is regarded as dangerous.

A PHOBIA AS TO FLYING. Phobias can develop in adult life
as well as in childhood. At one of the Hypnosis Symposiums where professional men are taught the use of
hypnosis, one of the attending physicians was used as a
demonstration subject to show how the causes of a phobia
could be uncovered.

Dr. Johnson stated that he had been a combat pilot during the last war, had had several missions but had survived
and had enjoyed flying. Once he had almost been shot
down but had managed to land his plane safely. After his
discharge from the service he had not had any occasion
to fly for some time but in taking a commercial flight had
become panic stricken in the plane. Since then he had not
been able to enter a plane and did not understand this
fear after having been a pilot himself. Significantly, as it
after developed, he termed his condition claustrophobia—
the fear of being in an enclosed place.

By ideomotor answers to questions it was brought out
that a past experience which had been frightening was the
basis for the phobia. This was quickly located. It was not
a repressed memory. Under hypnosis he was regressed to
the experience and taken through it four times.

After the war ended he was ordered to fly from a Texas

airfield to Seattle where he was to be discharged from the Air Force. His squadron was to make the flight under the command of a major, Dr. Johnson being a captain. While flying over Idaho a bad thunderstorm was met with. The other members of the squadron wanted to fly around the storm but the major ordered them to fly though it as gas was low and they would have had to go some distance to pass around it.

The storm was much worse than expected. The planes lost contact with each other. Lightning was flashing continuously and Dr. Johnson feared it might hit his plane. He was buffeted terrifically, was finally caught in a great downdraft and as he came out of it one of the wings of the plane developed a bad vibration. Finally he lost all control of the plane and parachuted to the ground, being badly tossed around on the way down. Later he found that two other pilots had had to bail out. One pilot had been killed when his plane crashed into a mountainside.

After being rescued and proceeding to Seattle by train, Dr. Johnson had been discharged without ever flying again. He had never thought of this experience as having anything to do with the phobia; however, questioning showed that it was the main cause, and his earlier experience in almost being shot down, a secondary cause. While being regressed to the experience he showed great fear and emotion but after going through it several times remarked that he felt greatly relieved.

A few months later Dr. Johnson wrote that he had bought a plane, obtained a private license and was enjoying flying again.

The doctor had not repressed this memory but had never connected the experience with his fear of flying. To avoid thinking about it he had decided that his problem was claustrophobia, but he actually had no fear in other places where he was shut in. This is rather typical of how the subconscious will avoid something very unpleasant and frightening and will rationalize to direct attention away from it. Although it was not brought out in the limited demonstration time, I would think it probable that some other frightening experience may have also been concerned as a cause—such as having been dropped while a baby. If so, apparently enough was accomplished to end the phobia by bringing out the precipitating cause. My suspicion as to this is based on the fact that phobias usually relate to some childhood experience.

## SUMMARY

Fears may be quite normal, but sometimes are abnormal and when extreme and irrational are phobic. Dr. Wolpe's method of desensitizing can be accomplished readily with self-treatment and is better applied to fears rather than phobias. You are quite likely to be the uncomfortable possessor of some phobia, for they are common. Most are not too disabling; the situations where they develop can often be avoided. Some may be extremely annoying and handicapping. If you have claustrophobia and cannot enter an elevator, you will do much stair climbing. Their development is usually related to some childhood fright, often with other related experiences.

Phobias are often easily overcome with the methods given you here. Locate the causes by your questioning technique. With self-hypnosis regress yourself and go through the experience several times until you have worked off the emotion tied up with it. This desensitizes you and you should lose your phobia. Always remember before regressing yourself to ask your subconscious if it is all right for you to go back to it. It is seldom that an experience is so horrible that it cannot be borne, but such is possible. Probably you would not be able to reach it, in this case, but such a question is a safeguard which should be utilized. Most fears and phobias can be handled with self-treatment but a phobia might be too deep-seated and professional help would be needed.

# Chapter 13

# KEEP SLIM AND YOUTHFUL
# WITHOUT DIETING

Emotional and psychological factors can produce a wide variety of ailments. Here we can only consider some of the more common ones. It is not always clear why the same factors may bring on an illness affecting the skin in one person, the digestive tract in another, a respiratory condition in someone else, and so forth. Let's take a look at one 'of the most common situations—overweight. It is not to be classed as an illness, but usually is an emotionally caused condition.

**That extra poundage.** The problem of overweight is usually one of overeating. In all cases, combinations of reasons and motives will be found to be present. Overweight may be a matter of only a few pounds or, with the grossly obese person, as much as a hundred or more. Usually a few pounds are easily shed, once the decision is made to reduce; excessive overweight is something else again and may be a deep-seated neurotic problem requiring therapy.

On the physical side, there may be a glandular condition which should have medical treatment. Physicians have said that glandular malfunction is a cause in only about two percent of overweight cases. More recently, indications are such that this is thought to be much too small a percentage. A glandular condition may exist, too, as the cart, not the horse, in that it follows from the overweight.

To be rid of a few pounds may safely be undertaken

with no need for medical treatment, using any sensible diet, plus autosuggestion, and applying plenty of determination to the process. Here in this chapter we are concerned with the individual who has much weight to lose.

Diet will sometimes bring loss of weight to the desired extent even if neurotic factors have brought on the overweight condition. If treated by a physician, the patient is given anti-appetite pills, possibly a diuretic drug to remove excess liquids, is put on a strict protein diet and is told to use self-discipline in eating. The diet is supposed to be low in calories. In most cases the patient loses for a while, then stops dieting and returns quickly to the former weight. If dieting is continued and there is a real loss of weight, a year later the patient is probably back to the same overweight condition. Very seldom is the loss of weight maintained, and frustration usually results. The reason is that the symptom is treated, not its causes. Removal of the reasons for overeating is an essential part of any successful treatment.

With the goal of considerable weight loss by self-therapy, you should be under the care of a physician for advice as to the rate of reduction which is safe for you as an individual. He can give you some anti-appetite pills which may help at first. One part of your job is to learn the reasons why you overeat. With elimination of this need, the excess weight will come off, though changing your eating habits is another indispensable part of your program.

**Why do people overeat?** The causes or reasons for overeating vary in individuals but some are invariably present in all cases. Eating tends to be compulsive and is not to be controlled by will power and self-discipline. Overweight people often say they seem to have no will power. It is not lacking. It simply is not strong enough.

In the development of obesity, the earliest cause for overeating goes back to infancy. When an infant is uncomfortable it usually is hungry. Feeding brings comfort and the baby feels good again. Eating is then subconsciously associated with feeling good. The conditioning of the child is like Pavlov's dog. With the dog the bell was associated with food. The infant associates food with feeling better.

When an obese person is upset, he heads for the refrigerator. "If I eat I'll feel better." Such a thought is not conscious but the inner mind compels such action.

We find the same or a similar association in the case

of smokers. To a child, sucking the thumb gives oral satisfaction. The smoker substitutes a cigarette for the thumb. The motive or need in smoking is exactly the same as with the thumbsucking child. The smoker believes smoking will relieve nervous tension, will quiet his nerves. Temporarily it may, but nicotine increases nervous tension thereafter. Soon another cigarette is needed.

Considering our seven most frequent causative elements in connection with excess weight, we take motivation first. What purpose does it serve? If a woman dislikes sex, she may unconsciously make herself sexually unattractive to her husband or to men in general (frigidity). Then she can escape from the sexual situation. On the other hand, if deprived of normal sexual satisfaction, a woman with normal sexual feelings may substitute stomach appetite for sexual appetite.

A compulsive desire for sweets often enters when this is true. Lack of love as distinguished from sexual love may bring the same result. Parental rejections as a child may turn the child to overeating to make up for the feeling of being unwanted.

If a parent is overweight, the element of identification may enter. There may be a hereditary tendency here, but more likely, an unconscious desire to be like a parent.

One of the common causes for overeating is a suggestion picked up in childhood by the subconscious. "You must eat everything on your plate." "You mustn't waste food." "You can't have your dessert until you've eaten everything." "You must eat to be *big* and strong." There may be other similar statements which have been repeated over and over again. Most children go through stages where there are eating problems which worry parents. This brings forth such remarks in concern over the child.

Feelings of inferiority and unworthiness can be a factor in obesity. The body image of oneself may preclude an attractive appearance. Self-rejection results and perhaps self-punishment.

In self-treatment these things must all be explored, with investigation of any past experiences which may have led to the ideas and emotions which promote overeating. Suggestion is an important part of treatment.

You do not have to diet! In reducing it is best to avoid dieting as such. To the overweight person, diet is a nasty word. He knows all about diet, has often tried it and after losing a few pounds has given it up. The thought

of dieting provokes resentment and resentment in turn
brings rebellion. No one likes·to diet; it is a nuisance. In
self-treatment, forget diet. You are not going to diet but
are instead going to change your eating patterns.

You have taste buds in your mouth so you will enjoy
food, as nature intends. Some foods are enjoyed more
than others, but most taste good. You can enjoy everything you eat, but concentrate on protein foods and avoid
the types which are most fattening, such as carbohydrates,
animal fats and sweets. According to Dr. Herman Toller
(*Calories Don't Count,* Simon & Schuster, New York),
unsaturated fats should be used, avoiding the saturated
ones (animal fats). He recommends eating the least possible amount of carbohydrates in controlling weight.

Resentments about diet can be eliminated if you realize
that no one is forcing you to diet or lose weight. If you
wish, you could gain instead, but that is not sensible nor
is it what you want. You are going to reduce because it
is the wise thing to do and it is what you desire. Do not
feel that you must never eat a piece of candy nor have
a sweet dessert, but you will indulge only rarely. You are
not to deprive yourself, you merely will change the kinds
of foods you eat.

**Write out your reasons for wanting to reduce.** Motives
for reaching a proper weight are important. It helps to
impress this on the subconscious by writing out your
motives. First and foremost should be the matter of
health. All statistics show that the greater the overweight,
the shorter your life will be. People sometimes eat themselves into the grave, digging it with a fork. Overweight
puts a continual strain on the body. If you had to carry
thirty or forty pounds of weight in each hand all day,
how tired you would become. The body wears out faster
under continued strain.

Another motivation should be personal appearance.
Everyone should try to look one's best with whatever
assets in appearance he has. In some Oriental countries,
plumpness in a woman might be considered an element of
beauty, but it is not an ingredient of beauty in Western
countries—it is quite the opposite.

Plain, everyday comfort is desirable. The overweight
person is far from comfortable, physically or mentally, and
is handicapped in many ways.

**How to change your eating habits.** In regard to taste,
the obese individual almost invariably, though unconsciously, bolts his food, chews but little and hurries through

the meal. Take your time when eating, retain each mouthful longer and chew it so as to get the full flavor of the food. When you do this, you will find that you seem to require less.

Most of us tend to eat everything placed on the plate before us. When eating at home, see that you are served small portions of all food. If still hungry, you can have seconds, but you will seldom want them. Restaurants always serve large portions. In dining out always leave a little on the plate. Do not feel that you will offend the hostess by not eating everything served you when you are a guest.

Eating between meals is a habit of the overweight individual, with a fourth meal before going to bed. Of course one of the best ways to cut caloric input is to stop this custom. If really hungry between meals, which may mean your blood sugar is low, eat something of low calory count.

**The red flag method.** An excellent way of reminding yourself not to snack is to place a piece of red cloth or paper on the door of the refrigerator, fastening it on with Scotch tape. At any time but meal-time this is a red danger flag. Let the door stay closed!

While reducing, there is a tendency to note progress by stepping on the scales each day. This is not recommended. Weigh only every week, or better, every other week, and always weigh at the same time of day.

The amount of food absorbed by the body will differ in individuals if one person eats exactly the same food to the calory as is eaten by another. One will lose and the other gain. Differences in activity and exercise would not account for all the disparity. In giving yourself suggestions about reducing, the subconscious can be told to regulate absorption so you take in less energy from the food you eat. You are to absorb only as much as is needed to maintain a weight of twenty-five pounds less than your actual weight. It is not scientifically certain if the subconscious can control the rate of food absorption in this way, but it is a possibility, since control of other body processes by the subconscious can be demonstrated.

When using suggestion in controlling the overeating tendency, emphasize your motives. Establish a goal—the ultimate weight you wish to attain—and determine that nothing is to stop you from reaching it. Use visual imagery with your suggestions. If you are aware that any emotional upset can drive you towards the refrigerator, the tendency can be counteracted. Sometimes in your progress there will be setbacks, some overeating, and a resultant gain of two or three pounds. Do not allow a temporary setback to discourage you. You may never have one, but if you do, regard it as only temporary and continue towards your goal. When it is reached eventually, you can maintain proper weight by occasional suggestions and awareness of keeping appetite controlled.

**Other digestive disturbances.** Our emotional troubles are often reflected by disorders in the digestive tract, including peptic ulcers, nausea, constipation, diarrhea, colitis, gastritis, hemorrhoids, and even tooth decay. Still other conditions may be psychosomatic. This makes quite a lengthy list. Fear upsets the functioning of any part of the tract. When we are frightened, the stomach "knots," the digestive process halts and, with extreme fear, there may be defecation. Chronic fears interfere with normal digestion in many ways.

Peptic ulcer is most prevalent in a definite type of person. He tends to be a worrier, a go-getter, aggressive and competent, having great responsibilities and facing them adequately. He is often an executive in high position. Physicians also tend to develop ulcers (cardiac conditions, too, are common with physicians). While the ulcer patient outwardly shows these traits and in his business life is adult in behavior, at home he is probably quite different, very dependent and even infantile in the way he acts.

The late J. A. Winter, M.D., comments (*The Origins of Illness and Anxiety,* Julian Press, New York) on these opposed characteristics. He makes a comparison, pointing out that the infant takes small frequent feedings as does the ulcer patient. Both are fed milk and soft, strained foods. Both are petulant and complaining when thwarted in any way, or when hungry. Sympathy and attention are demanded. With the ulcer patient there is a conflict between his need to accomplish and be adult and also to remain a child.

**Nausea and what to do about it.** One of the ways the subconscious tries to handle anything unpleasant, frightening, or threatening is to eliminate it from the system. This can be accomplished in the matter of physical things by vomiting or by bowel movements, diarrhea aiding the latter process. If tainted food is eaten, the stomach rejects it in both directions. The subconscious mind may endeavor to do the same thing with ideas or situations which are objectionable. This fails, but the effort is continued. The result is chronic nausea or chronic diarrhea which may become colitis. Unfortunately, the subconscious can be illogical in its reasoning and pays no attention to end results. It seems to think if these measures fail at first that continued effort may succeed.

MARION'S CASE. A young woman had suffered for some months from chronic nausea. She was unable to retain food; she had even been hospitalized three times and fed intravenously, and had lost much weight from malnutrition. After such a spell in the hospital, her physician referred her for hypnotherapy as the situation was desperate and other treatment had failed. At a conscious level she was quite willing to be hypnotized but resisted unconsciously and could not even enter a light trance.

She was seen daily for several sessions. Suggestions helped her retain some food and she began to gain a little weight and feel stronger, but still had bouts of nausea at times. She had no conscious insight into the reasons for the condition. With pendulum questioning, Marion, as we will call her, brought out that there was a past experience which was the original basis for the illness. Another recent incident had precipitated it. At first no more could be learned about these events, because of great resistance. Suggestion was impressed on the subconscious as to the danger in her situation. After a few visits she was able to bring the causes to consciousness.

Often there seems to be an original cause for a symptom in some past experience but it lies dormant until a similar, related incident occurs. This precipitates or activates the symptom. This was so in Marion's case.

When Marion was fourteen, her father suffered heavy financial losses and was in great difficulty, with the possibility of having to close his business. Their home was heavily insured and he remarked one day that he wished it would burn so he could collect the insurance, which would save his business.

Marion heard the remark. With the desire to help her father, she thought about the matter for a time and decided to act. While her parents were absent she heaped kerosene-soaked papers in the living room under the window curtains and set them on fire. She ran out, closing the doors, as the room blazed up. Then her conscience made her think better of the plan so she ran next door and called the fire department. Fire trucks quickly arrived and put out the fire with no great damage.

Marion had forgotten her little pet dog when she set the fire, not noticing it asleep in the living room. Smoke and lack of oxygen suffocated the dog. Marion's heart was broken and on seeing the dead pet, she vomited. Her guilt was extreme—she had killed her pet. She was afraid to confess to her parents.

The precipitating cause—the bell for her conditioned reflex—was when her husband bought a dog and brought it home. It was the same breed as the pet she felt she had destroyed. Marion became hysterical and vomited again. The nausea became chronic, triggered by seeing the dog daily. She also was trying to eliminate from her system the unpleasant memory and the guilt feelings over her childish act of setting fire to her home.

When the girl understood the reasons for her condition, discussion assuaged her guilt feelings somewhat. It was suggested that she tell her parents about her original experience, on the basis of confession being good for the soul. She was told she had punished herself enough for a childhood wrong. Her plan had failed in that only enough insurance had been collected to repair the house. Marion's husband was financially well off and when told of the situation, volunteered to reimburse the insurance company the amount paid, some $1000. This helped relieve Marion's guilt still more and her nausea was ended.

**Constipation.** Like that of sleeping pills, the sale of laxatives and mineral oil is enormous. Constipation plagues millions of people. It becomes a habit and sluggish bowels must continually be stimulated. The reasons for development of the habit frequently go back to childhood and the period of toilet training. One of the ways a child can resist a demanding mother without being punished is through withholding when placed on the pot. Mother urges and is upset when the child does not comply. It is a safe way of thumbing the nose at mama. A later bowel movement in the diaper is also a way of thwarting or getting even with mother, giving her unpleasant work to do. The habit of withholding is set up and continues perhaps throughout life.

A different kind of need to withhold may also be present which is related to miserliness. Psychoanalysts believe the feces are unconsciously associated with money. Insecurity and financial fears can then cause withholding of the feces, just as the miser or person who is "tight" with money holds on to it. There is even a relationship here in the word *tight*.

Withholding as to the bowels and the accompanying tightening of the rectal muscles can also result in the formation of hemorrhoids. Tension over other emotional matters also is evidenced by tightening of the rectum. This condition often becomes aggravated following a period of great stress or emotional upset. Surgery may become necessary.

## SUMMARY

If overweight is a problem with you, and if you wish to reduce, your first step should be to learn the subconscious factors causing the condition. This can be done with ideomotor questioning and then you can begin a program of reduction by following out the means described here. The problem is overeating, the overweight resulting. You do not need to diet or count calories, although you must change some of your eating habits and patterns.

Stomach ulcers, nausea, constipation and other digestive tract ailments have been discussed and if any of these conditions are present with you, you should be able to overcome them with self-treatment. Of course you may require medical treatment also.

*Chapter 14*

# NEVER SUFFER FROM HEADACHES AGAIN!

Medical reports state that more than three million people in this country suffer from migraine, mostly women. Chronic headache of other types is probably even more frequent. Of course almost anyone can have an occasional mild headache. Since headache in one form or another is such a common matter, we should deal with it here. The symptoms are described here so there can be a better understanding of their causes.

Migraine is one condition where it seems that a certain type of person may develop the illness. There are exceptions, but the woman sufferer from migraine tends to be small, petite and with a good build. The male type is almost the opposite, big, strong and husky—the football player type. On the psychological side, both sexes are perfectionists and both are outwardly non-aggressive to an extreme degree.

Migraine is marked by violent headaches experienced on one side only as a rule, with the eyeball on that side becoming painful and sometimes protruding. Vision is affected by this. Accompanying the headache will be nausea and vomiting, sometimes diarrhea. At times migraine has been called "sick headache." Prior to the onset a kind of visual aura is noticed.

The headaches sometimes seem to follow a pattern and come on certain days of the week or after a definite interval of time. This is not always true and they may come only rarely or every few days. With women, they often accompany menstruation. The extreme pain of the head-ache, together with the stomach upset, is often incapacitating and the sufferer goes to bed in a darkened room, quite unable to function.

**The why of these headaches.** There are several common denominators in almost every case of migraine. The victim is outwardly placid, even-tempered, and non-aggressive as well as being a perfectionist. Inwardly things are different! Since women are much more likely to have migraine than men, we will use the feminine form here. The woman with migraine is full of unrecognized, bottled-up hostility, rage, frustration and resentment which cannot be expressed or even admitted to. These are looked on as unacceptable emotions which should not be felt and must be suppressed. A comparison might be made to a steam engine. When too much pressure develops, it blows off through a safety valve. With migraine, the headache seems to be the safety valve. When these emotions build up, the headache comes.

Because these emotions are unacceptable and intolerable, guilt feelings over them bring a need for self-punishment. The headaches serve this unconscious purpose admirably. They are most painful and distressing. Other sources of guilt may also be present calling for self-punishment. When the headaches accompany menstruation and possibly in other situations, guilt due to sexual inhibitions may be involved. However there is also a physical part here, with endocrinal changes during the period.

The perfectionist must do everything just so. Clothes must be hung up in their place; shoes arranged neatly. A few dirty dishes in the sink is unthinkable. Ash trays must be emptied as soon as soiled. Furniture must always be in its designated place. Cleanliness is essential. Otherwise she feels uneasy and uncomfortable and she is compelled to make the necessary adjustment to end the disorder. A picture hanging unevenly must be straightened at once. The emotions of frustration and resentment toward anyone (usually the husband) who upsets the perfect arrangement of things are additional factors promoting the headaches.

A migraine patient usually denies the existence of these emotions. It does little good for a therapist to point out these factors to the patient, but she can be led more subtly to a realization of these facts. She will say she does get angry at times, and she well may, with extreme cause for anger, but it is a rare occurrence. She cannot admit to feelings of rage and hostility, for these emotions are wicked.

There are drugs which at times control migraine, but they may only modify the headache and rarely are completely effective. They should be taken when the first advance symptoms show up, for the person always knows they are beginning, unless they start during the night. Often drugs are taken without result. Drugs treat only the symptom and not its causes.

The migraine patient must be led to see how bottled-up emotions produce the condition. In my treatment of such a case with hypnosis, I find it of advantage to the patient to bring about an attack during the office visit. This can be done by regressing her to a time when she had a less severe attack. I do not want to subject her to a bad one. When it appears, I let her feel it for a few moments, then bring her back to the present, causing it to disappear. This will convince the most skeptical patient of the causes being emotional rather than organic. It shows that the headache can not only be evoked but can also be controlled.

**Migraine can be a family characteristic.** Migraine seems to run in families, but it is not certain if heredity plays any role. There may be some constitutional tendency, however. But a child will pick up character traits from a parent, perfectionism for instance, and will identify with the parent. If mother has migraine, dramatization with the effort to be like her may call for migraine attacks. Perfectionism is usually taught by parents. Punishment and scolding for showing temper leads the child to believe that anger and hostility are wicked emotions which must be stifled.

The migraine patient is invariably overcontrolled. When she cannot control environment, she feels threatened and panics, but cannot do anything other than suppress her emotions, due to the compulsion to control. It is a vicious circle. Hostility is feared for this reason. If control is lost and aggression shown, there may be dire consequences with rejection brought on oneself.

Perfectionism is a symptom of insecure feelings about oneself as a person, bringing on feelings of inferiority which in turn produce frustration and rage. Environment must be controlled to feel secure. But other people are involved in environment and it cannot always be controlled. The migraine sufferer is also neurotically very sensitive. A disparaging remark will be taken to be aimed at her when there is no such intention. She will blame herself needlessly for many things, invoking still more guilt. "It's all my fault" is her attitude.

**How to treat the condition.** In treating migraine, whether with self-help or otherwise, uncovering the causes and changing some of these attitudes is imperative. To overcome the perfectionist trend I sometimes ask, "If as a child your mother knew that one reason for your headaches is because of your need to be perfect and to do everything just right, do you think she would demand such behavior from you?" I urge a break in the pattern. "Go home and mess things up a bit. Make it a point to leave some dirty dishes in the sink sometimes. Be sure not pick up immediately after your husband, if he leaves his clothes around. You can keep things clean without having to whisk away every spot of dust. Modify your perfectionist drive. Do not try to eliminate it. You can be comfortable if you satisfy only 90 per cent of this urge, which you can accomplish, rather than to try for 100 per cent, which can't be done and which then brings frustration and guilt."

Ways of venting anger and hostility have been described. The migraine patient should make it a point to recognize that these emotions are normal, not evil ones. When they are stirred up, instead of suppressing them they should be recognized and discharged. This must be in some acceptable way. It is more difficult for a woman to do this than for a man. She should be able, however, to find some sport or exercise which will serve. Or she can go into her bedroom and beat on a pillow with her fists. She can express her emotion by talking about it, and can do it nicely without quarreling.

Self-treatment should include these adjustments. Also, check our seven basic keys with pendulum answers to questions. If drugs are being taken to control the condition, at first cut down on the dosage as progress is made, and then gradually end all medication. If migraine is an accompaniment of menstruation or of premenstrual tension, a physician can prescribe drugs, diuretics, which will relieve this and will serve to remove one cause of the headaches.

If there is some pattern as to the appearance of the headaches, there is probably some association to a past experience which is causing them to appear at that particular time. This can also be explored by our questioning technique.

The migraine victim is not likely to want to regress herself to a past headache since they are dreaded. If they can be ended without this, the regression should be avoided. Nevertheless, learning that you can produce and then eliminate one is most helpful.

**Other types of headache.** Many different conditions can produce headaches, with either organic or psychological causes involved. We might class as the "garden varieties" those such as fatigue, eye strain, and psychological headaches which merely serve as an alibi to get you out of something you do not wish to do. Headaches may accompany colds, influenza, fevers and still other illnesses. As a symptom they may be a warning, just as other forms of pain call attention to something wrong. Frequent or chronic headaches call for medical diagnosis.

When a diagnosis has been made, medical treatment of the condition may be needed. Even when the cause is organic most headaches may readily be relieved with hypnotic suggestion. This might not be true when there is some strong neurotic need for the headache. With few exceptions, a headache results physiologically from an engorgement of blood in the area. Since the subconscious can control circulation, suggestion can bring subsidence of the congestion and the headache will dwindle away. This is symptom removal, as is taking aspirin, but it is safe and can end the discomfort.

**Self-treatment of the chronic headache.** Self-treatment of chronic headache should be through finding the underlying causes, as with all psychosomatic ailments. It should not be undertaken until medical diagnosis has shown that the headaches do not have some organic cause, For example, it would be folly to try to end headaches caused by a brain tumor or some other serious condition.

The seven basic factors should be investigated when self-treatment is applied. One of the most frequent of these causes is found in organ language—the phrase "That's a headache to me" operating to produce a real one. Any unpleasant situation, experience, or idea may serve to stimulate this idea and the headache itself. More than one of the seven keys probably will be implicated. Since headaches are painful, there may be a self-punishment motive.

When dealing with a headache by suggestion, after hypnotizing yourself your suggestions might be about as follows: "Within a few moments my head can begin to clear. The excess blood will begin to drain back into my body, allowing the congestion in my head to be relieved.

The discomfort will soon lessen and soon the headache will be gone."

The suggestions should be repeated two or three times. When they have been given, divert your thoughts, try to become busy at something so you do not think of the headache.

WHY JOHN D. HAD CHRONIC HEADACHES. John was a forty-three-year-old house painter who had been afflicted with chronic headaches for several months. They had increased in frequency and intensity until they were being experienced three or four times a week, always beginning during the night. Sometimes they would be so bad that he would awaken and scream with the pain.

No organic reason could be found for the condition and drugs had little or no effect. A neurologist recommended a lobotomy operation (cutting into the brain) as the only means of controlling the pain. Such an operation often leaves the patient like a zombie or vegetable. In desperation John was ready to submit to this but the family physician told him first to see if hypnosis could help.

While there are types of headaches which appear at night, these had been ruled out. Appearance at night was an indication of some psychological cause, as the neurologist should have known. John was sure the basis for the headaches was physical but hoped suggestion could stop them.

During treatment questioning with the pendulum went as follows:

Q. Sometimes our emotions influence our bodies so we have physical reactions and it is just possible your headaches have some emotional cause. Your inner mind knows if this is true. Of course it may not be so, but let's find out. Is there some emotional reason for the headaches? (The pendulum gave the signal for *yes*. John seemed surprised and exclaimed at this, but remarked that it must be so, in view of the answer. This was acceptance of the idea.)

Q. We can feel guilty about things we do, even about thoughts we may have. We all do things we regret. Is this a punishment for something?

A. *Yes* (pendulum).

Q. Do you feel guilty about something?

A. *Yes.*

Q. Is it about something definite rather than for ideas or general guilt feelings?

A. *Yes.*

Q. The headaches began about a year ago. Possibly you feel guilty about something that happened long ago, or it might have been just before you first had the headaches. Was it something recent, within the past three years?

A. *Yes.*

Q. Was it within two years?

A. *Yes.*

Q. Was it within a short time before the headaches began?

A. *Yes.*

Q. Does this have anything to do with sex? (The pendulum moved diagonally, not in one of the four usual movements. This could mean perhaps or that the question was not worded so it could be answered affirmatively or negatively.)

Q. Evidently the question was not clear. Did you do something you considered sexually immoral?

A. *Yes.*

Q. Was a woman involved?

A. *Yes.*

Q. Was it your wife?

At this point the patient said his wife had died a few months before the headaches appeared and he had since remarried. They had begun shortly after his marriage. This statement was taken as a clue.

Q. Does it have something to do with your present wife?

A. *Yes.*

Q. Tell me verbally about your wife's death.

John said she had been ill for a long time with cancer of the cervix and finally died. He had met his present wife about a year before the first wife's death. They had had an affair. He did not feel good about this but he had been unable to have intercourse with his wife for some time. He related that he was in love with the other woman and had married her just six weeks after his wife died. The parents of the first wife had reproached him for this and he had felt very guilty about it.

Q. Are the headaches a punishment for that?

A. *Yes.*

Q. You believe in an afterlife. If your former wife knows you are happy with this girl and are married again, what do you think she would say about it if she could tell you?

A. She told me I should marry again. She might have thought I should have waited a little longer, but I think she would have told me to go ahead.

Q. Do you think she would want you punished in this way?

A. *No* (verbal).

Q. Is there any other reason why you have headaches?

A. *Yes.*

Q. Is it something else calling for self-punishment?

A. *No.*

Q. Is it related or connected with some experience of your past?

A. *No.*

Q. Does it have something to do with your environment?

A. *Yes.*

Q. What is bothering you in your present situation aside from the headaches?

A. (Verbally) Well, I'm broke. My first wife's illness took all the money I had saved. I make pretty good money painting, but with these headaches I haven't felt like going to work lots of days. I'm all worn out from them in the morning. So I've missed a lot of work. The money situation sure is a headache to me!

Q. Is that why you have real headaches? Is the situation a headache to you and then you produce a real one?

A. *Yes* (pendulum).

Organ language was explained to John. He was then hypnotized and given strong reassurance. He was told his financial situation could quickly improve with the ending of the headaches. An affirmative answer was then given by his fingers to the question as to whether he could now be free of the headaches, now that he understood the reasons for them.

There had been only two sessions with John. A third brought out that his first wife had suffered from migraine. His headaches, though not migraine, were therefore an appropriate punishment for his guilt. John had not had a headache since his last visit and six months later was still free from them. The combination of organ language and a need for self-punishment was the key to the headaches.

## SUMMARY

Before attempting self-treatment of headaches a medical diagnosis certainly should be made, though most types could be stopped temporarily by hypnotic suggestion. Common sense calls for knowledge of the possible physical causes.

With migraine, if you are unfortunate enough to be so afflicted, you may not feel that some of the character traits described here are present with you. Perhaps not all of them are. Some you probably will realize do apply to you. If you are doubtful as to others, question yourself with the pendulum. You are most likely to doubt whether the remarks about repressed hostility are present in your case. You will almost certainly find that they do apply to you. Above all, you must learn to accept such emotions as normal and not bad, and to find some acceptable way of venting them.

With other types of headache self-treatment is not usually difficult. Seek the causes. The garden variety are often easily stopped with hypnotic suggestion. You do not even have to investigate causes. Chronic ones can also be stopped in this way but will be permanently ended when you find the reasons for them and make some emotional and mental adjustments.

With a little study of the cases cited in the various chapters, you can learn how to ask the necessary questions to locate causes.

# Chapter 15

# THE KEY TO A HAPPIER
# SEX LIFE

It has been estimated that there are more than three million cases of migraine, about the same number of recognized alcoholics and as many more unrecognized. When it comes to sex problems, it is impossible even to guess at the number of cases of frigidity, impotence, homosexuality, perversion, and sexual inhibition.

In the field of gynecology, it probably would be true to say that most women are affected at least occasionally with female psychological disorders such as painful or difficult menstruation, infertility, abortion and various other conditions. Space prevents consideration of more than the most common, but treatment of all would be much along the same lines.

Dr. Cheek believes that menstruation difficulties are always psychological in origin regardless of when they occur and of whether or not an organic condition is also present. Menstrual cramps may stem from several of our seven factors—self-punishment, identification, conflict over sex, avoidance of intercourse as a motive, and especially as a result of suggestion.

When a girl reaches puberty she often has heard discussion of the "curse," of how painful it can be, and thus is led to expect menstruation to be painful. Then that is almost sure to follow. The same effect of suggestion is found in morning sickness of pregnancy. When a woman's friends learn she is pregnant, they will inquire, "Have you had your morning sickness yet?" Most women expect to have it. While the endocrine system is upset by pregnancy, nausea is not a normal part of that condition. It is almost unknown in women of native primitive races. Simpler cases of dysmenorrhea and nausea can usually be controlled merely by suggestion, coupled with an explanation of the part played by suggestion in bringing on the condition.

THE REASONS FOR RUTH'S PAINFUL MENSTRUATION PERIODS. The most severe case of menstrual cramps in my experience and that of the referring physician was Ruth R., 28 years old, married to a man with an identical twin brother. The physician had resorted to morphine to stop the pain and she always spent two days in bed at her periods, suffering greatly in spite of the drug.

At a conscious level Ruth remembered hearing of the cramps before she first menstruated and had had mild pains during each period. It had become much worse after she grew older. Finger responses to questions brought out the reasons. Questioning went like this:

Q. Is there some other reason for this condition besides the effect of expectation and suggestion about it?
A. *Yes* (finger).
Q. Is there some conflict over sexual relations?
A. *No.*
Q. Are you identifying with someone else who had dysmenorrhea?
A. *No.*
Q. Is there some past experience, or more than one, associated with the cramps?
A. *Yes.*
Q. Is there more than one incident?
A. *No.*
Q. When did this happen—was it before you were fifteen years old?
A. *No.*
Q. Was it before you were twenty?
A. *Yes.*
Q. Was it between eighteen and twenty?
A. *Yes.*
Q. Was it when you were eighteen?
A. *No.*
Q. At nineteen?
A. *Yes.*
Q. Was it a sexual experience?
A. (Verbally) Yes, I know now what it was. I remember. I had my first affair at nineteen. I felt awfully guilty but kept

on, as I liked the boy a lot. About three months after we had been going together I missed my period. I was a week late and was really frantic. I was sure I was caught. One night I got down on my knees and prayed God to make me menstruate. I told him I didn't care how much pain I would have, just let me not be pregnant.

Next morning she had begun to menstruate. The extremely painful periods followed from then on. Asked if she really thought a miracle had happened, she smiled and shook her head. It was pointed out that she had not actually been pregnant at all and her pact with God had not been necessary. Then she was asked with finger responses if she could now be free of the pain when she had her periods—if she had had enough self-punishment. The finger reply was that she could.

RUTH—A YEAR LATER. About a year later Ruth made another appointment. She had had no further difficulty until her last period, which again had been extremely painful. She was asked if she had done anything about which she felt guilty, but declared she had not. "I thought of that," she said, "but couldn't think of anything at all." With more finger questioning the story was different.

Q. Are you punishing yourself again?
A. *Yes.*
Q. Have you done something you shouldn't?
A. *Yes.*
Q. Have you been untrue to your husband?
A. *No.*
Q. Is there something else you feel guilty about?
A. *Yes.*
Q. Is it about sex?
A. *Yes.*
Q. Something must have happened. When was it, shortly before your last period?
A. *Yes.*

It was then suggested that a thought would pop into her mind as to what this was about (she was in hypnosis).

"Oh," she said, "it must have been my brother-in-law. That's it! He has often made passes at me, but I would never have an affair with him and told him so. One night, though, when my husband and I were having intercourse I thought it might be interesting to pretend it was his brother instead, just imagining it. I did and it was quite exciting. I didn't feel guilty about it, because it wasn't real." (This was rationalizing to soothe her conscience.)

Although consciously not aware of guilt, her subconscious regarded this as worthy of punishment, hence her cramps had returned. With insight and a decision to do no more such fantasizing, she had no more difficulty.

Many other menstrual conditions are on an emotional basis also. Frequent periods may be a means of escaping from sexual relations. Cheek had found rejection of femininity involved in sterility, in habitual miscarriage, vaginal atrophy, vaginitis, and in frigidity.

**The frigid woman and the man who can't.** In all sex problems there basically is inhibition, confused and faulty thinking, and fear. Fear is the great destroyer. It is an emotion intended by nature to protect and preserve us, but is perverted through false ideas into the exact opposite. It causes unhappiness, ill health, and even death, instead of functioning as nature intends. Ridding ourselves of irrational fears is the main aim of all psychotherapy.

Even today most children are brought up with little or no instruction about sex. Parents are usually too embarrassed and inhibited over sex themselves to explain it to their children. Never having been told of menstruation, the first period with its bleeding can be frightening for a girl and many have this experience. With childhood conditioning that sex is wrong, dirty and that a girl must not let a boy touch her, it is not surprising to find so many women frigid. Statistics show about one in three to be partially or totally frigid.

Sex is so often considered immoral that the meaning of the word *moral*, if it is mentioned, means sexual morals. Actually, the word refers to many other character traits and behaviors and is general rather than specifically about sex.

With normal curiosity about the body, children wish to know why the other sex differs physically. Examination and investigation with another child is likely to meet with severe punishment and threats from a horrified parent. Sex becomes tabooed and is regarded as evil and dangerous. Growing up and maturing may bring a conscious change in thought about sex but to the subconscious mind sex is still wrong. Marriage makes no difference. Fear has been instilled.

Today in polite society it is permissible at times to speak of sexual intercourse. A few years ago this would have been a vulgar social error. However the word *masturbation* must never be mentioned, even if we have lost some of our Victorian attitudes. We retain the ostrich attitude toward this subject. It must be ignored as something bad and perverted. Guilt over masturbation and mistaken ideas about its effects are main sources of sex troubles.

SHE BELIEVED SHE WAS CRAZY. A twenty-one-year-old girl, whom we will call Helen, visited a psychiatrist. She was greatly disturbed and nervous. Helen had given up her position as a secretary due to her emotional condition. She told the psychiatrist that she should be committed to an institution and asked that he do so. When asked why, she insisted that she was insane. He tried unsuccessfully to reassure her and, as he had a full schedule, sent her to me.

Her story soon came out. At the age of ten her mother caught her masturbating and punished her severely, told her of the evils of "self-abuse" and took her to their family doctor. Physicians are not always founts of wisdom and may have false ideas about sex themselves. This physician, to whom she gave prestige and regarded as an authority, told her if she did not stop the practice, "By the time you are grown you'll go crazy." This idea is common but has no basis at all in fact.

Helen had continued to masturbate, having a strong sex drive, but with great guilt and fear. Now she was twenty-one and grown up. The doctor had said she would go crazy and she had become more and more disturbed thinking about this. Her disturbance and agitation confirmed his statement. She must be crazy.

Explanations correcting the ideas installed in her quickly relieved her mind. She had had boy friends but had been afraid to have sex relations or to fall in love and marry. About six months later she phoned that she had just been married and was quite happy.

**Treating sex problems.** In treating sex problems it is always advisable to have the patient, whether male or female, obtain one of the good books about sex and marriage and read it. Any bookstore can recommend one. With a married couple it is best to take turns reading such a book aloud to each other and to discuss the information in it. This helps remove false ideas and inhibitions.

Masturbation is a natural urge when there is no opportunity for obtaining more normal sexual satisfaction. When unmated in captivity, any animal, even birds, will masturbate at certain seasons. Of course they feel no guilt about it. Such guilt is confined to humans and is a conditioned reflex.

In the animal world also the female is only interested in sex during her ovulation period and permits no approach except at that time. With humans this is not true. Nature obviously intends sex to be enjoyable for a woman at any time. Fear and inhibitions block the intention of nature.

Some frigid women dislike the sexual act and submit because they feel it a marital duty. Others find it mildly enjoyable but never have a climax. Still others do, but rarely. Some may dream of sex and have an orgasm but only in dreams.

**Men have sexual troubles too.** Frequently the difficulty is not in the woman but lies in the ignorance or inhibitions of the husband. The wife is not actually frigid but is not properly stimulated. In this country a man likes to imagine himself to be the great lover—sexually adept. It is surprising how few men are good lovers, contrary to their own opinion.

Often with little or no sex play in advance, the sex act is over in a moment or two. A woman needs time to become sexually aroused and with such a situation has no chance to reach a climax. Many men who are always premature believe this entirely normal and would be astounded to be told it is a form of impotence. If this is overcome, the apparently frigid wife can respond normally. Too often the measure of sexual competency in men is frequency—quantity rather than quality.

The Casanovas, the Don Juans, the "wolves" among men continually look for new fields of feminine conquest. They brag of these and boast of their sexual prowess. Under the surface, with this type, is doubt and uncertainty of their ability. It is continually necessary to prove how good they are, without ever satisfying the doubt.

The Kinsey report on sex habits showed that the average length of time in intercourse in this country is between five and ten minutes. A similar investigation in France gave the average time as over half an hour. Apparently it is no myth that Latins are good lovers.

While men in general are less inhibited than women as to sex, they have had much the same experience in childhood of learning that sex is wrong and wicked. They may have been told that if masturbation is practiced they will not be properly capable of intercourse. This idea is prevalent and has no foundation in fact. Expectancy acts as a suggestion and impotence may follow.

The Freudian theory of a "castration complex" is sometimes a factor in impotence. Freudians believe all males and some females go through a period in childhood where this complex is functioning. Normally it is lost in growing up but frequently it persists. The term castration is hardly correct, for it really is a fear of damage to the sexual parts. A boy caught masturbating may be punished and threatened, "If you ever do that again I'll cut it off." Such a remark can well produce the complex. Other fears of damage through sex relations may be held.

Both men and women tend at times to make a parental figure of the marriage partner. In marrying men often unconsciously seek a mother; women seek a father. Unconsciously identifying the spouse with a parent then makes sex relations incestuous. This is never consciously realized but may be an important matter in either frigidity or impotence.

**Sexual blocks and their causes.** One of my cases was quite unusual. It was a young man, husky and athletic, married to a beautiful girl with plenty of sex appeal. In three years of marriage they had had intercourse six times. The strange factor in this situation was that the husband had strong desires and was physically quite able but rarely could bring himself to do more than make love a bit. He was not impotent but completely blocked at having intercourse. Questioning with the pendulum went like this:

Q. Is there any fear which prevents you from having sex?
A. *No.*
Q. Is it because you feel sex is dirty and wrong?
A. *Yes.*
Q. Is there any other reason for the trouble?
A. *Yes.*
Q. Is it related to some past experience?
A. *No.*
Q. Do you tend to place your wife in the position of being a mother to you? Is she a mother figure?
A. *Yes.*

Here the young man explained that he was raised by an aunt after his mother died during his infancy. His wife resembled the aunt in many ways.

Q. In regarding your wife as a substitute mother, does sex then seem wrong?
A. *Yes.*

Further questioning with verbal replies as to sex being
wrong and dirty brought out that he admired the wife
greatly and respected her. To him it seemed degrading
for such a fine person to be subjected to intercourse. He
wanted her, but it would soil and debase her. Nice girls
should not be interested in sex. A most unusual situation
was presented here.

With women, rejection of femininity, not necessarily
homosexual in any way, may cause difficulty as to sex.
Envy of men's advantages in this world can block the
normal sex drive. If there is strong unconscious resentment of men, or fear of them, frigidity may be a means
of frustrating and thwarting the man, even though he may
also be loved. Fear and resentment may have been
aroused through real or fancied rejections, perhaps first
by the father, and because of previous love interests which
were not returned. Another common source of resentment is seen with an attractive girl who has had to fight
off the advances of men and continual attempts at seduc-
tion. Such a woman will remark, "All men are beasts.
Sex is all they want!"

Sometimes in both impotence and frigidity the condition is not present with a sexual partner other than the
mate. Inability is gone with someone else. Here interper-
sonal relationships between husband and wife would be
acting as causes. This might include resentments and perhaps the fact that as we grow older we become sexually
less attractive. There may be less desire with proximity
and becoming used to the mate. With someone else the
case is different. In that of a man with a younger and
more beautiful girl than the wife, sexual stimulation
would be much greater and impotence would disappear.

The element of expectation and doubt, with the law
of reversed effect again in operation, is a consideration in
sexual blocks. When there has been trouble in the past to
achieve an erection or an orgasm, if the person "tries
hard" there will be no result.

**How to maintain emotional balance.** The emotional
balance in sexual matters is very delicate for both men
and women. Sometimes fatigue, worry, or some minor
emotional upset may cause difficulty which should be only
temporary. Few men have failed to have such an occurrence. Alarm and fright with failure to appreciate the
reason could then subsequently block the sexual impulse.
Impotence might become chronic.

Soon after the last World War a young naval officer

was discharged from the service. Although married, during two years in the South Pacific he had had an affair with a naval nurse and had had many pangs of conscience over it. He eagerly looked forward to living with his wife again but on arrival home found himself quite impotent, to his mortification. He had arrived home after a long trip, tired and worn out but had felt he should please his wife with intercourse after his long absence.

Alarmed and worried he consulted a psychologist when he failed again and again. As the cause was quite superficial, matters were soon remedied. It was explained that his fatigue was a part of his difficulty on the first night home. Guilt and self-punishment were involved. While it might have been inadvisable if the wife had not been a well-adjusted person much in love with him, the young officer was urged to confess his transgressions to her. After doing so he was forgiven and thereafter had no further difficulty.

**Old age and sexual vigor.** A common belief among men is that old age brings great loss of sexual vigor. While this is true to some extent, diminished sexual ability with increasing age is much less than is believed. If such an effect is expected, it surely will happen, but many men in their eighties are able to perform well. "It's all in the mind" is at least partially true. In one survey as to sex, an eighty-two-year-old man was queried as to frequency. He replied, "Why every night. Doesn't everyone?" Undoubtedly he should have a gold medal!

**Technique for the impotent male.** Unless impotence and frigidity are very deep-seated neurotic manifestations, these conditions are not difficult to correct with insight into causes. Wolpe offers an excellent technique to be followed by the impotent man. The principle is such that it should also be effective in frigidity.

With the wife informed of the purpose and her cooperation secured, even though it may be difficult for her, the husband is told to engage in prolonged love-making in bed but with the understanding that there will be no intercourse. He is to enjoy the sensations aroused and to become as stimulated as possible but to refrain from consummation even if able. This amounts to a pact with the subconscious—I can enjoy sex up to a point but no further. With the idea that the act itself will not be indulged in, inhibitions are removed to that extent. When this "exercise" has been carried out a few times and he finds himself more and more able to proceed, he is told he may.

With accomplishment, his doubts fade and the ice is broken. With a woman unable to reach a climax, the same method should be employed.

Women seldom realize that the muscles of the vagina can be consciously controlled and contracted. Dr. Arnold Kegel has found the teaching of muscular control and its practice during intercourse will often end frigidity where the causes are superficial.

Homosexuality, sexual perversions and some other conditions are unlikely to be helped with self-treatment and hence are not discussed here. Their treatment should be with a skilled psychotherapist. These mental ailments can be treated successfully provided the patient wishes to change. Too often there is no such desire.

## SUMMARY

The woman reader of this chapter should now have a better understanding of the sources of some menstrual disorders. If you have been bothered with menstrual cramps and no organic reason for them has been found, you should be rid of them readily by applying the self-help methods you now have at your command. Check with questioning if you are responding to suggestion, and with hypnosis root them out by countersuggestions. Tell yourself that you no longer need expect them and can be free of them in future. Check for guilt feelings about sex and possible self-punishment.

Any woman with frigidity as a problem would do well to read one of the various books on successful marriage and sex life. Overcoming wrong thinking about sex is a most important part of self-treatment for this condition. You should explore for possible early childhood experiences about sex, possible sexual experiences with other children or even with adults which may have been repressed from memory. Have you any hidden fears about sex? Locate what they are—the kind of fear. Realize that nature intends sexual relations to be enjoyable. Search for any reasons for guilt about it. Has masturbation a part? Does fear of pregnancy enter the picture?

For the impotent male much the same course should be followed. Either sex may be identifying the partner with the parent of the opposite sex. I think this is apt to be more likely with men. They often tend unconsciously to make a mother figure of the wife. One of the strong factors in impotence is the expectation of difficulty when some impotence has been displayed. Almost anyone could have difficulty at some time, as when greatly fatigued, and in some other situations. Guilt over an affair could call for self-punishment to produce inability. Most men would be annoyed by such an occurrence but would realize that it can happen and is unimportant. If greatly alarmed by it, fear may develop that it will happen again and the expectation is a suggestion that it will. There's that old devil, the law of reversed effect going into action again! Get rid of the expectation—"so what" can help.

To combat this situation Wolpe * offers a technique which is excellent. With the cooperation of the wife, who is to be told the purpose, make love to her but without consummating the act. Even if you find yourself able and eager, you should hold off. Follow this procedure three or four times or until you realize that you are quite able to carry out the act satisfactorily.

* Adapted from *Psychotherapy by Reciprocal Inhibition* by Joseph Wolpe, M.D., with the permission of the publishers, Stanford University Press. © 1958 by the Board of Trustees of Leland Stanford Junior University.

# Chapter 16

# MASTER YOUR EMOTIONS
# AND OVERCOME ALLERGIES

Of the many psychosomatic ailments to which the human race is prone, the common cold is the one most frequently encountered. The term *common* is most appropriate. More man-hours of labor are lost because of colds than from any other illness. There are few, if any, of us who do not have an occasional cold.

A great deal of research has been conducted as to colds, with a very small amount of knowledge resulting. The cold is still a mystery to physicians. Its symptoms are almost identical with those of influenza and some other diseases. This leads to the virus theory as their cause, and certainly colds may be "catching." Apparently there are different types of colds and some may be created by a virus.

Some of the popular beliefs about colds have been proved wrong by research. Getting the feet wet, becoming chilled, being in a draft will not cause a cold. Though they may if you think they will! Any highly emotional experience can produce a cold. When a child becomes angry or disturbed, sniffles may follow. Perhaps the symptoms are an imitation of crying. Coughing, draining sinuses, a runny nose, the accumulation of phlegm may all be an attempt to eject something from the body in the same way as does nausea. Some colds may serve the purpose of getting us out of something we dislike to do. A cold can keep a child from school, an adult from going

to a job he dislikes; or it can be an alibi to escape from
some other unpleasant situation.

The cold may be a way of expressing some emotion
such as grief or self-pity. Sinusitis, chronic inflammation
of the nose and hay fever all have similarities in symp-
tomatology and may be the expression of an emotion.

Psychotherapists sometimes will deal in one session
with a patient entering the office with a bad cold. If unconscious motives and reasons for the cold are uncovered,
recovery may take only a very short time and the patient
may leave without a symptom. There could be no virus
at work in this case.

**Allergy and its causes.** The whole matter of allergy is
as mysterious as the causes of colds. We may be sensitive
to pollen, dust, or almost anything, even including another
person in rare cases. In England a woman was granted a
divorce because she was allergic to her husband and any
contact with him resulted in the appearance of a rash!
But why are we sensitive to some things? Domestic animals can suffer from allergies as do the humans with
whom they are associated, but I have heard it said that
wild animals are never known to have an allergy. This
would indicate that allergic reactions are a product of the
stress of modern living, although the resulting condition
is a physical one.

The oft repeated story told to show the psychological
factors present in allergy is that of the man allergic to
roses. Whenever he saw a rose he would sneeze, his nose
would run, his eyes water and an allergic attack was
precipitated. One day he entered a room where there was
a bunch of beautiful roses in a vase, and an attack
promptly started. It ended quickly when he learned the
roses were artificial!

ALLERGIC TO IMAGINARY ROSES. In one of the courses
offered by Hypnosis Symposiums, which are given to
teach physicians, dentists and psychologists how to use
hypnosis, one of the instructors undertook to induce hypnosis in the entire group of those taking the course. He
began by asking the "students" to close their eyes and to
visualize a vase on a table before them. Then they were
told to put an imaginary yellow rose in the vase, to see
it and smell it. One of the physicians who was following
these instructions promptly began to sneeze, to gag, and,
wiping tears from his eyes, rose hastily and left the room.

A little later he returned and was asked to come to the

platform and be a subject for a demonstration of the
treatment of an allergy such as he had displayed. He commented on his surprise when he reacted to a purely imaginary yellow rose. The use of the pendulum in questioning
the subconscious was explained and his movements of
the pendulum were established.

Q. There is some reason for your allergic reaction to roses.
Is it all right for you know what it is?
A. *Yes* (pendulum movement).
Q. Are you allergic to all roses?
A. *No.*
Q. Only to yellow ones?
A. *Yes.*
Q. In such a condition there probably is an association to
some past experience. Is this true in your case?
A. *Yes.*
Q. Is there more than one incident involved?
A. *No.*
Q. How old were you when it happened? Was it before the
age of fifteen?
A. *Yes.*
Q. Before five years old?
A. *No.*
Q. Before ten?
A. *No.*

The age was then found to be at ten through further
queries.

Q. Was this a frightening experience?
A. *Yes.*
Q. Was any other person present?
A. *No.*
Q. Where did it happen, outdoors rather than indoors?
A. *Yes.*
Q. Was it at home?
A. *No.*
Q. Was it at school?
A. *No.*

Further questioning located the scene as the farm of
his grandparents. Dr. N. was then hypnotized and told to
return to the experience. He had been riding a horse bare-
back when the animal became frightened and threw him
off into a patch of yellow roses. Thorns had scratched
him badly, mostly on the face, and he had been frightened
at the blood and pain. He caught the horse and, as he
mounted again, the horse began to eat some of the roses.
Dr. N. picked one himself and ate the petals, wondering

if a rose would taste good since the animal seemed to like them.

When he reached the farmhouse, a reaction set in and he became nauseated. He cried and sniffles started. After relating this story, finger answers to more questions indicated that there was no other reason for the allergy. Sight of a yellow rose was by association the trigger mechanism which set off the allergic attack. Roses of other colors had no such effect. He was then asked if, with understanding of how this old childhood event had affected him, he could now be free of the reactions to yellow roses. The answer was that he could.

At this point one of the other physicians in the audience left the room and came back shortly with a yellow rose he had found in a flower shop in the building. The allergy victim was asked to smell this, which he did very gingerly. There was no reaction at all, to his great relief.

Next morning Dr. N. came to the class and said he had had an interesting time the night before. For years he had been bothered with claustrophobia and became panic-stricken when in any confined space such as a closet or elevator. Intrigued by the demonstration of the day when he had lost his allergy, he decided that night to see if he could uncover in the same way the cause of his phobia. With pendulum answers he questioned his subconscious. In this way he learned of having been locked in a dark closet at the age of five by an aunt, in punishment for some act. He had been locked in until he became very frightened and had screamed until released.

Dr. N. had forgotten the incident but recalled it when he learned from the pendulum what was involved. As his allergy had ended with insight into its cause, he thought perhaps he would no longer have his fear of enclosed places. Leaving his hotel room, he rang for the elevator, of automatic type, and rode it up and down several times without feeling fear.

The conscious mind may be totally unaware of what is behind an allergy, a phobia, or other condition. The subconscious part of the mind knows exactly why it has developed. Sometimes resistances prevent bringing out the causes as quickly as is seen in the cases given here. Without resistance they are usually located by questioning in a very short time. They can be found with other methods, such as free association, but the time needed is far, far longer. A bit of study of the way questions are asked, as in the cases cited, will show you how to ask suitable ones in self-treatment.

SHE HAD TO CLEAR HER THROAT CONTINUALLY. Marjorie had always wanted to be a singer and when younger had studied voice and been told she would have a career. She was thirty-five when I saw her, bitter and sullen, hating her job. Her career had been ruined when at twenty-two she developed a need to clear her throat every few minutes. No organic reason could be found causing this, and no treatment helped. She continued hacking and clearing her throat. She had never married.

Marjorie hoped hypnosis could help her. Someone had told her it might. She expected results in a session or two and angrily said she could not afford more treatment than that. Not knowing how long it might take to help her, she was taught how she could explore the reasons for her condition herself by using the pendulum. Its movements surprised and interested her.

Two weeks later she returned smiling and in an entirely different mood. Her symptom was gone. She wanted to tell me about it. It was an interesting story.

Living in the Midwest at the age of twenty-two she was engaged to a young man whom she loved greatly. On a holiday they had gone canoeing together on a lake. When she tried to change her position in the canoe it had upset, throwing both of them into the water. She could not swim and her fiancé was not a good swimmer. He managed with much struggling to pull her to the upturned canoe to which she held. Then, exhausted, he sank and drowned. She was rescued a few moments later by others in a rowboat. She had swallowed much water, choking and sputtering and coughing.

With her self-questioning she had located this experience as the cause of her throat clearing. Her guilt feelings were strong, believing her carelessness had caused the death of her fiancé. Because of this she had never married. Self-punishment also made it necessary for her to be unable to follow her career as a singer.

She had decided that all this was no longer necessary, taking an adult view. She stated that she now intended to marry a man she was going with, and her symptom had disappeared completely.

**Asthma and self-treatment.** This condition can be chronic and merely uncomfortable or so severe that the sufferer can die from inability to breathe during an attack. To the patient, asthma can be most frightening when he struggles helplessly for breath. Medical treatment can help the condition—drugs which relax the bronchial spasms, thin the mucus. Hormones such as cortisone and ACTH also may be effective. However, drugs treat only the symptom, not the causes.

Difficult breathing in the asthmatic may be on inhaling or when exhaling. When questioned as to which is his pattern, a patient is probably unaware of how he acts during an attack. He has to think about it and note which is involved. If he is watched closely, other actions and behavior are seen during an attack. Respiration will be at a fixed rate, certain movements and attitudes are seen. Fear symptoms appear—perspiration, rapid pulse, trembling.

If you are troubled with asthma, you are probably in the care of a doctor, but self-treatment can certainly be helpful. If you plan this these side effects should be considered. One way of breaking up the asthma pattern is that recommended by Dunlap for breaking habits. While free from an attack, you should go through the movements and other actions you have noted as present in an attack. These should be carefully studied so you know what they are. Try to reproduce them, all of them, exaggerating them as much as possible. If this should bring on an attack, it will be mild and it teaches how one can be produced intentionally and also how one can be controlled and ended.

**Is asthma an allergy?** Few asthmatics are able to cry. Questioned about it, they are surprised to learn this about themselves. Asthma has been said by psychiatrists to be a suppressed cry. They have also said that in all asthma cases there is some conflict centering on the victim's mother. This goes back to childhood and the suppressing of crying at that time is involved. Another psychiatric theory is that there has been something the child wanted to tell his mother but has failed to confess it, usually some transgression.

In treating asthma, I have asked the sudden, unexpected question sometimes, "How old are you?" while the patient is wheezing. Often the answer has been "eight," or some other childhood age, much to the surprise of the patient. When this happens, it indicates a spontaneous regression or association to some experience at the stated age. This can then be investigated further.

The relationship with the mother is shown by child asthmatics when they are taken from the home environment. At a California sanitarium for asthmatic children, most of them recover quickly when they have become used to the sanitarium situation and are away from the mother. Returned home, attacks frequently recur. With such child cases, an entirely different attitude and behavior on the part of the mother, and also the father, may bring relief.

In defense of the theory that asthma is an allergy, it has been pointed out that very young babies may have the disease. This is true, but babies have emotions just as do adults. The asthmatic is expressing emotions by his condition. He can learn this truth and intentionally develop other ways of expressing them, venting anger and hostility, as the migraine patient must learn to do, learning to cry and to avoid the side reactions and behavior patterns which accompany the attacks.

CASE OF THE ASTHMATIC PSYCHIATRIST. An asthmatic psychiatrist, Dr. S., became a patient after he had taken a course in the use of hypnosis and realized its value in psychotherapy. Although he had had many hours of psychoanalysis, his asthma still persisted. He was a very good subject.

Questioning brought out some of the reasons for the condition. Most, but not all of them, were already known from his analysis. They followed some of the patterns mentioned here. During his eighth session, while in hypnosis, questions were asked and finger replies made as follows:

Q. You have learned some of the reasons why you have had asthma ever since childhood. Let's find the original cause, the first experience in your life which has anything to do with causing the breathing difficulty. The very first thing. How old were you at the time? Was it before five years of age?

A. *Yes* (with finger movement).

Q. Was it before three?

A. *Yes.*

Q. Before two?

A. *Yes.*

Q. Before your first birthday?

A. *Yes.*

Q. Was it before you were six months old?

A. *Yes.*

Q. Was it before three months of age?

A. *Yes.*

Q. Before one month?

A. *Yes.*

Q. Could it have been just after you were born?

A movement of a fifth finger followed, indicating that the question was not clear or too vague.

Q. Did something happen at your birth that has to do with this?

A. *Yes* (The movement of the finger was repeated several times as though for emphasis.)

At this point the psychiatrist made the comment, while still in hypnosis, "That's certainly strange. No one remembers being born. It's ridiculous. My subconscious must be kidding us!"

Q. Was the experience involved frightening?

A. *Yes.*

Q. Is it all right for you to recall it?

A. *Yes.*

Q. Is there in your memory remembrance of being born?

A. *Yes.*

The partial type of age regression was now invoked and Dr. S. was told to go back in time to just before he was born. He told of feeling wet and cramped and exclaimed at how vivid were his impressions. Told to go on through the experience of being born, he began to show signs of great discomfort. His face became fiery red, he choked and coughed, gasped that he could not breathe. A moment later he took a deep breath and said, "The doctor is holding me up by the heels and he just smacked me on the rear. Now I can breathe!" He seemed much relieved and the flush began to subside from his face.

Asked to go through this experience again, his reactions were much milder. He went through it twice more and then was asked,

Q. Is this difficulty in getting your first breath the origin of your asthma?

A. *Yes.*

Q. Now that you have learned this and know the other things which are a part of the picture, can you be free of the asthma?

A. *Yes.*

After being awakened, Dr. S. discussed his experience, saying he was convinced it had been a real memory and not just a fantasy. He was much impressed and felt a tremendous relief. He believed his emotional reaction was such that no fantasy could have produced it to such a degree. He remarked that psychoanalysis could never bring out such an early memory. Following this session, Dr. S. had had no further attacks.

In this situation there was no suggestion made that birth might be the origin of the asthma. The questioning did not suggest it in any way, but the patient's subconscious mind brought it out spontaneously as being the original cause.

**The birth experience as original cause.** Following this same procedure the same thing has happened in several other asthma cases seen in my work. Seven patients with chronic headache have also given the birth experience as being the original cause. With these, delivery by means of forceps seemed to be very painful and responsible for a headache at the time of birth.

In my opinion these are actual memories, though scientific proof would be difficult. If forceps delivery were confirmed by the mother or the obstetrician, the patient might have been told of this instead of actually remembering it. Several psychotherapists who use hypnosis have also found birth to be one of the causes in asthma, headaches and also in the rejection of femininity, where the mother has expressed regret at her baby not being a boy.

**A look at allergy.** The body may react to allergic stimuli with a respiratory condition such as asthma, or hay fever, sinusitis, or still other ailments. An allergy to some food may bring a digestive upset. The skin may be affected by pollen, dust, or some other stimulus. Like so many illnesses, allergies seem to result from conditioned reflexes which have been set up.

Treatment, aside from medical, should include locating the source of the conditioned reflex and the reasons for the allergic reaction. Almost invariably some past experience will be found behind an allergic digestive disturbance. This may have been when a certain food caused an upset stomach in childhood. The upset may merely have accompanied the eating of the food and not have been the food itself. Being told some food is not good to eat will act as a suggestion. A few generations ago no one would eat tomatoes because they were believed to be poisonous. Eating a tomato with this belief in mind undoubtedly caused nausea or diarrhea in many people.

**The skin.** In a former book of mine, *Techniques of Hypnotherapy* (Julian Press, New York), a part of the volume consists of articles on the use of hypnosis in various medical specialties. One is a splendid article by Dr. Michael J. Scott of Seattle on "Hypnosis in Dermatology." This is condensed from a complete book written by him on this subject.

According to Dr. Scott, many skin conditions arise from emotional or psychological causes. He cites a long technical list of conditions where this is a possibility. Causes are similar in all of them, regardless of the form taken by the skin condition. Sometimes the actual cause is organic but the ailment is exaggerated because of emotions.

Suggestion may be used to bring relief, although it does not deal with causes. Itching can be modified or prevented by suggestion and healing speeded. For centuries suggestion has been used for the removal of warts. It may be indirect, as when some ointment or medicine is applied to the warts. With the expectation that it will remove them, they fade away. With children a wart will usually disappear if it is "bought" from the child. He can be told, "You have a wart there. Perhaps you don't want it. You know, I make a collection of warts. Would you be willing to sell it to me? I'll give you a dime for it." With the purchase completed, the child is told it is no longer his and he cannot have it any longer. Within about two weeks' time it will probably be gone.

Where there is "weeping" in a skin condition, it may be a substitute for crying, just as is true in asthma. The suppressed emotion causes the skin to break out and "weep."

In dermatitis and other forms of skin ailments with itching and weeping, two factors are frequently present. These are in the nature of organ language. Both were involved in the following case.

HOW BETTY'S RASH WAS CLEARED. A dermatologist asked me to visit his office and see a patient of his, a seventeen-year-old girl named Betty. She suffered from an extreme case of neurodermatitis, her entire body covered with a red, weeping, itching rash.

Betty's mother had agreed with reluctance to the use of hypnosis for her daughter when the physician mentioned it. She wanted to be present but was told she must remain in the waiting room. The mother was obviously domineering, overprotective, and treated the girl like a small child. Betty was good-looking but dressed in unbecoming clothes, not such as teen-agers wear, and had on cotton stockings.

She was a good subject and readily went into hypnosis. Told she could talk without awakening, this was said to her in a positive tone—"Something is irritating you. What is it?" Betty sat up and opened her eyes, though staying in hypnosis. "MOTHER!" she exclaimed, bitterly. "It's my mother. She treats me like a little girl. I can't do anything other girls do. I can't dress like them. Look at my clothes, my hair. I've never had a date. I can only go to parties if my mother is along. It's mother!"

Betty was encouraged to talk further of her troubles. She told of being forbidden the use of cosmetics and of other taboos. Organ language was explained to her and it was pointed out that her skin was the external part of her, exposed to outside influences. Her mother was irritating her by her actions and so she had brought on an actual skin irritation. Also she was itching to do things forbidden her. She was told to substitute in her thinking the word *annoyed* for *irritated, wishing* instead of *itching*. Since she could now understand the sources of the dermatitis it was suggested that her skin could return to normal, with a change in her environmental situation which we were sure could be brought about.

The dermatologist then discussed the situation with the mother. She was upset when told her overprotectiveness and her undue restrictions were the reason for the daughter's skin condition. She readily agreed to change her ways, to accept the girl as almost an adult, to let her do what other girls her age are allowed to do. Within a month Betty's skin was clear and normal.

The organ language noted in this case is not uncommon in others. Irritation and itching as used in this way in our language may be main factors in skin ailments. There can be many other causes, such as masochism and identification. Freudians believe itching and the resultant scratching may be a substitute for masturbation, which seems farfetched, but may be true at times. If allergy is concerned, the reasons behind the allergy should be sought.

## SUMMARY

If you are one of those who suffer from any of the conditions mentioned in this chapter, the case histories should be helpful to you in clearing it up. Procedure should be as you have now learned. Continue any medical treatment you may be having, but unfortunately many physicians who deal with these types of illness are not psychologically oriented and ignore emotional possibilities as causes. A joking remark is often made by other physicians about dermatology as a medical specialty —the patient never dies, never gets well, and the doctor never has night calls to make. Physicians who are aware of the emotional problems in these ailments, like Dr. Scott, do treat them successfully.

One great advantage in using hypnosis with a skin condition where there is much itching is that it can frequently be used to control scratching and hypnotic anesthesia can control the itching, itching being a mild form of pain.

# Chapter 17

# COMMON AILMENTS AND
# HOW SELF-THERAPY HELPS
# YOU REMEDY THEM

Psychosomatic problems involving the muscles or bones are as frequent as those of the respiratory or digestive tracts but orthopedic specialists seldom refer such patients for psychotherapy, usually being oriented organically. A slipped disc is much more likely to be treated surgically than psychologically.

Dr. Wayne Zimmerman, of Tacoma, Washington, is one orthopedic surgeon who is well aware of the part played by emotions in this area of body physiology. As he says, "The mind and the body cannot be dissected and do not function separately, one from the other." One of his interesting cases is described here as being quite unusual. It shows a way of affecting the subconscious mind which can sometimes be helpful when resistance is met with. It is summarized from an article by Dr. Zimmerman, "Hypnosis in Orthopedic Surgery," in my book *Techniques of Hypnotherapy.*

**Conscious insight into causes isn't always necessary.** A woman patient had suffered a shoulder dislocation seven times within a period of a year. An operation was finally necessary to correct the condition. A year later bursitis developed in the shoulder (inflammation of the bursa, with a calcium deposit), and the bursa was taken out surgically. Later the same shoulder again troubled her, but no reason for it could be found.

Suspicious of some emotional reason for these recurring shoulder conditions, Dr. Zimmerman resorted to finger movements in answer to questions. He asked if there was an emotional factor causing the trouble and the *yes* finger responded. The next question was, "Is this something you can discuss?" The *no* finger moved. Apparently the matter could not be brought into consciousness. This is a situation most frustrating to both patient and therapist, blocking progress.

The surgeon then told her to relax completely and to focus on the problem so she could get it into view. She began to cry and showed much emotion but did not know why. She could think of no reason. She was reassured and again asked if the cause could now be described. The answer was again negative.

Dr. Zimmerman then instructed her subconscious mind to concentrate and work on the problem. It was to be worked out at a subconscious level. In the meantime, the inner part of her mind was to keep the shoulder comfortable so she could carry on her work. The subconscious agreed to this, as indicated by a finger reply. No cause of her shoulder trouble ever came to light but there was no further pain and she could use her arm normally.

This illustrates an important point. Emotional difficulties are centered in the subconscious and it has full knowledge about them. With proper prodding by suggestion, it can understand and integrate matters. Its viewpoint can be altered without conscious insight ever being gained. This is in contradiction of the Freudian theory that only through conscious insight can a condition be remedied. While it certainly is always best to bring such knowledge to awareness, it is not essential. This is shown by Dr. Zimmerman's case, also by my own experience and by that of others. When resistance prevents insight, this method may succeed in bringing a change. It may fail if the resistance is too strong or if the motivation for a symptom is too great for the subconscious to give it up.

**Arthritis—and what can be done about it.** Here we have another very common ailment and again one which is a medical mystery. Organically, the possible causes are many—vitamin or food deficiency, viruses or bacteria, "focal infection," as from the teeth, glandular disturbance, and still others. Various drugs have been used in treatment, also bee venom, ultrasonic vibration, and hormones

such as cortisone and ACTH, with hormones sometimes
giving good results.

Arthritis in severe cases is exceedingly painful, always
so to some degree, with the swelling and rigidity of joints
or of the spine. Affecting the knees, the patient may be
unable to walk. Sometimes arthritics are completely incapacitated.

There seems to be something of a character pattern
with this disease. Like migraine victims, arthritics tend
to be hostile, resentful and aggressive, but bottle up these
emotions. The personality is often rigid and inflexible and
perhaps this is psychologically reflected in the rigidity of
the joints. The sufferer has been vigorous and has compulsively driven himself to accomplish.

A possible motive for the illness might be its use as
a means of putting on the brakes to such a drive, through
fear of failure or for other reasons. The condition serves
this purpose. There can be a fear that uncontrolled temper may get one into trouble. Conflict develops over the
desire to hit out at fate, or at particular individuals,
mixed with fear of the result of doing so, and guilt
because of such a desire. Self-punishment is often found
to be a factor.

WHY KAREN DEVELOPED ARTHRITIS. Karen was a woman
in her late forties, a European, very intelligent, a university graduate, and single. She spoke five languages fluently
and came from a former wealthy family which had lost
its money during the last war. During the war she had
worked in the intelligence service of one of our allies,
with nearly a hundred people under her supervision.

Karen came to this country soon after the war and
her savings soon vanished. She was not trained for any
work. Finally, in desperation she took a position as maid
to a wealthy woman. Her employer was an alcoholic and
a most disagreeable person, who could not keep servants
because of her rages and tantrums. Karen was unable to
save money, although fairly well paid, because her father
in Europe was ill and she had to send money home each
month.

Some months before I saw her, Karen had developed
a bad case of arthritis in her hands. The finger joints
were swollen greatly and were so painful that she could
hardly move her fingers. Her hands were clawlike; the
fingers bent so they could not be straightened. This inter-
fered with her work.

She had visited several doctors and had had different kinds of treatment to no avail. The condition grew worse. She had no thought of psychotherapy, believing the illness purely a physical one, but hoped hypnosis could control the pain.

Karen was much surprised when pendulum questioning was used and an affirmative answer was given when she was asked if there was some emotional cause for the arthritis.

On being encouraged to talk and tell of her history, she described her work and told of her employer's treatment of the servants, including herself. She wanted to leave but could not save enough to quit. She felt demeaned and resentful at being a servant after having been raised in wealth.

During one visit, in talking about her employer she exclaimed, "I hate that woman. I hate her! She's a bitch. I'd like to kill her—to strangle her!" As she spoke, she lifted her clawlike hand and reached out as though grasping someone. Then she looked at her hands and their position. "Oh!" she gasped. "That's why my hands are so crippled!"

Desire to kill her hated employer was a horrible thought. For holding such a wish, self-punishment was called for. Repressing and burying the emotion, being unable to express her anger, was one cause of the condition of her hands. It was symbolic—the fingers clutching at the throat of her employer. Another motive, which she brought out later, was an unconscious attempt to escape from the situation by making her hands crippled so she could not do her work.

Understanding gave her some relief and she felt much less pain after this. However, her environment was the same and Karen could do nothing about it. Not long after this she was taken to Europe by her employer. While there, the woman flew into a rage at Karen and discharged her, but gave her two months' wages and first-class plane fare home. By traveling economy class Karen returned with enough money to live on for a time. She finally found a suitable position where her knowledge of Europe and languages could be useful. By this time her hands were free from all pain and the swelling of the joints had gone down considerably. As a boost to her self-respect, the employer tried to hire her again and apologized.

**Other cases of arthritis and bursitis.** In other cases of arthritis and bursitis, repressed rage and the desire to hit or kick have been uncovered. The condition prevents such overt acts of hostility and also serves as punishment for having them.

As there is a physical involvement in these diseases, psychotherapy may not bring relief. A bursa swollen and inflamed from a calcium deposit may need to have the calcium removed. A rigid spine may not lose its rigidity or the deposits of calcium be absorbed.

**Slipped disc and backache.** In a magazine article, the quip was once made, "The most commonly used labor-saving device is the backache." It certainly can serve as an excellent alibi and also as a punishment. Tension may cause the tightening of back muscles and even be responsible for the slipped disc. This latter condition presumably comes from lifting too heavy a weight or from an awkward movement which causes the disc to protrude. Remembering how often accidents are subconsciously provoked, one must wonder if the movement which caused the strain or slippage of a disc may have been intentional at a subconscious level.

With either a man or a woman, such a condition may have as a motivation the avoidance of sex. Low back pain often has some sexual problem behind it. Conversely, a motive might be to prevent the enjoyment of sex when there is a strong inhibition about it.

**Torticollis or "wry neck."** This is a peculiar condition which physicians seldom think of as related to emotions. Yet any possible physical cause is obscure and the few cases I have seen were all on a psychological basis. In torticollis, or wry neck as it is popularly termed, the head is turned to one side by a tightening of the neck muscles. It becomes impossible to bring the head to the normal position without great effort, or it may not be possible to turn it at all. Sometimes it is bent forward and down, rather than turned sideways.

With the neck twisted, the individual must move his eyes or turn his whole body in order to see in front of him. It is difficult or even dangerous to drive a car. The muscles become so taut that they are very painful. If the strain is prolonged, there will be atrophy of the muscles. Cure therefore is then much more difficult. It is a most uncomfortable condition. Medical treatment is with drugs to relax the muscles and with massage. As both treat only the symptom, it usually persists.

SHE TURNED HIS HEAD. I have found similar causes in three of the four cases of torticollis which have come to me. With the first I was at a loss and used only suggestion under hypnosis in trying to relax the muscles. It was a complete failure. Some years later a man visited me, his head twisted to the left almost at right angles. A businessman named Kelly, he had been to several physicians and had had drugs and massages but his neck was still pulled so his head was to the side.

Without going into details as to the ideomotor responses to questions, the causes were brought out, Kelly relating much of the story verbally. He was married, with a fine wife and several children. He had employed a most attractive secretary whose desk was at his left in his office. His business called for much social drinking and he may have been an alcoholic, although he would not admit it and claimed he could stop drinking at any time. He had never tried, nor did he wish to stop.

Due to close association with the secretary, Kelly fell in love with her, and she returned it. Being of the same religion and both very conscientious, an affair was unthinkable to them. Their religion forbade divorce. After several uncomfortable months with this relationship, they mutually decided that she should obtain another position and they would see each other no more. Kelly was shaken and emotionally upset, but the decision was carried out as being wise.

When the girl had left, he began to have trouble with his neck, finding his head turning always toward the left side. The strain became greater and greater, regardless of treatment. Eventually he could not move his head at all.

Organ language was working in this situation, with phrases I had never met with before. The girl had "turned his head" (to the left toward where she sat). He was "looking back" at their innocent affair with regret. As he also put it, with their decision made, "things took a 'turn.'" Another cause was self-punishment because of guilt over his mental infidelity.

When Kelly recognized these factors and organ language was explained, the neck muscles loosened and he could keep his head in the normal position, to his great relief. At his next visit it was again twisted to the side. He had been drunk the night before and awakened that morning with a hangover and his neck turned again.

Questioning showed that this was more punishment—for getting drunk. With some hypnotic suggestion he could bring the head back to position and left with it straight.

Kelly rarely became "tight" during the week but every Saturday he indulged and went to bed drunk. Each Sunday the torticollis was back and would persist for two or three days. Then for the rest of the week it would disappear. He seemed then to have had enough punishment for the time being. He realized the situation after the questioning, but declared he would not stop drinking. The last I knew his wry neck was still present intermittently, but he was free from it several days each week.

SHE HUNG HER HEAD IN SHAME. Wry neck is not a very common condition but the former and the one following are so interesting and unusual that they are discussed here. The next was a woman in her mid-thirties. Her head, instead of being turned to the side, was bent down so far that she was forced to tilt her body back in order to see. It was very painful to her. Self-punishment and another form of organ language again proved to be the causes.

She was married and had two children. Neither she nor her husband wanted more but she became pregnant again. He insisted on an abortion. Soon afterwards the torticollis developed. When I saw her it had continued for some months; all treatment failed to help.

I had learned something from the previous case and soon brought out the causes. She felt very guilty over the abortion, to which she had consented but with many misgivings and much guilt. Now she was "hanging her head in shame!" Strange what our subconscious minds can do to us.

## SUMMARY

In this chapter you have read of Dr. Zimmerman's case where he was unable to bring out any emotional case for his patient's shoulder condition but was able to cause her subconscious mind to review matters and evidently change its views so relief was gained. No conscious insight was developed. In your self-therapy you may find yourself blocked in some way at times and can perhaps resort to this technique with success. You should suggest to your subconscious, in such a situation, that it go to work on the problem, think it over and realize that for your betterment the condition should be ended.

While there are many possible physical factors in arthritis, it may also have emotional causes. As it is a painful matter, self-punishment may be involved. Your seven keys should locate any possible psychological reasons for the condition.

The torticollis cases will give you a better idea of how organ language can affect you.

# Chapter 18

# YOU HAVE THE POWER!

From the case histories which have been described, one might think that hypnotherapy is quickly and easily accomplished. When the causes of a condition are easily reached and the need or motive for it is not too strong, this may be true. At times there are failures. These may be due to strong resistances. It also may be that our knowledge of the mind and of illness is just insufficient.

The old admonition, "Know Thyself," is of utmost importance, but in some ways and at times it is difficult to gain the required knowledge. The methods given here for reaching an understanding of our mental processes and of the effects of emotions will help you to a better knowledge of yourself. Changes in thinking patterns, removal of conditioned reflexes, learning the sources of illnesses and of behavior all will help you to know yourself better. Such knowledge is the real key to happiness and good health.

Excellent progress in self-betterment may be had even if previous treatment for any situation or condition has not been successful or if there is doubt as to results. At times negative thinking may bring a temporary relapse which could be normal in the course of your progress. This can be instructive if the reason for the relapse is recognized. Further work will bring more progress. Avoid discouragement if there is a slip back; realize that it is only temporary.

WHY A SINGER WAS HOARSE. Things do not always go as

a therapist might wish when trying to help a patient. For example, a prominent male singer was referred to me because he feared he was losing his voice. For some time he had commanded high fees for his performances. Now he was badly frightened. When he talked, his voice was very hoarse. However, his agent said he still sang well and was able to perform. The singer believed his singing was "lousy" as he put it and he was much concerned over the situation. A clue was that it had persisted for almost three years. Why had he not sought help before, even if he now felt it was growing worse?

Richard, as we shall call him, was an excellent hypnotic subject. With finger movements information was brought out. He had been forced to have a tonsil operation three years before and at that time had been worried as to how the removal of his tonsils might affect his voice. I have since been told by physicians that it could not affect it at all. Something had happened while Richard was unconscious from the anesthetic during the operation. Some remark had been made which acted as a suggestion and brought on the hoarseness.

Under hypnosis he regressed to the operation. He told of a mask being placed over his face and what happened while he was "out." When the surgeon completed his work he had remarked to a nurse—"Well, that takes care of this damned warbler!" Presumably what was meant by this was that the operation was over. Richard's subconscious interpreted it another way. Worried beforehand about how his voice might be affected, this statement confirmed his fear. The operation would affect his voice badly. On his recovery from the surgery, the hoarseness appeared and had continued until the present time.

Following this session the hoarseness was gone. After being awakened he left, feeling happy and relieved, but another appointment was made in order to investigate further. When he came back a week later, the hoarseness was present again. He was dispirited and glum.

The reason for the relapse was quickly found. While driving to a performance, his wife had remarked on how strange it was for the hoarseness to have ended so suddenly. She had commented, "I can't believe you are over it. I'll bet it will come back." It did.

Evidently Richard was highly suggestible. Again he left with no hoarseness shown. I heard nothing from him for over a month. His agent then informed me of the situation. After a few days, Richard was hoarse again. He felt there was no use continuing treatment.

In studying the situation, it would be logical to suspect other causes for his relapses. He had found the symptom could be removed, at least temporarily. He now knew it had a psychological basis. Evidently some motivation or need for it persisted. Subconsciously he did not want to lose it and therefore rationalized that further treatment would do no good. It is a good illustration of how patients sometimes end treatment or perhaps go from one therapist to another. Consciously he wants relief but unconsciously needs to keep his symptom.

**Reviewing the ways for self-betterment.** Self-knowledge is not won without effort. The habits and attitudes you have acquired over many years cannot be changed overnight. Some things can be accomplished very quickly and ordinarily the time in self-therapy will not be long. The aims and purposes you have may be much different from those of some other reader. For this reason it is impossible to give specific directions to fit the needs of everyone.

Changing the way you think and handle your emotions may be all you will desire. Someone else may wish to accomplish this and also to overcome conflicts and other difficulties. The reader with a psychosomatic complaint will want to rid himself of the illness and be well. Behind all these aims is the desire for happiness and success.

Procedure would be similar for any of these situations though details will vary. Having read this volume, you have an understanding of how the subconscious mind functions. You have learned methods of affecting it to fulfill your goals.

The first step in self-therapy is preparation. Learn to relax, following the methods outlined. This will be valuable in many ways. As Dr. Wolpe pointed out, his patients made far better and faster progress when they had learned relaxation.

Relaxation will also aid in mastering autohypnosis. After reading about it, any previously held fears of hypnosis should have been lost. To repeat what has been said before, autohypnosis will hasten your progress and make it easier, but it is not essential in using the techniques which have been described.

Some of the self-help measures given are aimed at helping you develop confidence in yourself—ego strength —and rid yourself of inferiority feelings. If you suffer from stage fright you will wish to overcome it. In becoming successful, speaking to groups may be necessary.

One of my most interesting patients was the late screen actress Marilyn Monroe, who came to me at the suggestion of a mutual doctor friend. This was some years ago before she became successful. Marilyn had had several opportunities in motion pictures but when given a part had "muffed" it. The moment she had to speak a line or as soon as the cameras started to film a scene Marilyn was paralyzed with fear. She could not speak or move. Although very attractive and showing good possibilities, no producer could afford to use a person with such stage fright.

This invariably comes from a lack of confidence, and feelings of inferiority. Sometimes there is also an association to some childhood experience such as a school play or performance of some kind where the person forgot lines or was frightened.

These things were all true with Marilyn. She was seen eight times, soon afterwards was offered a good part in a screen play and found her difficulty no longer held her back. She soon went on to stardom and great success.

**Carrying out your program.** The natural tendency on the part of the reader will be to attack your worst problem or condition first, as that is what you are most concerned about. This is a mistake which can make your total undertaking much harder to accomplish. It is very important to begin with minor matters. Start by tackling some minor liability in your list of liabilities. After learning autohypnosis, the next step should be to assess yourself. You begin to change your self-image when you start with character changes and revisions in your ways of thinking.

If you have no particular emotional troubles but suffer from some psychosomatic illness, you can then attack its sources and causes. If such an illness is only one of other serious problems, it should be left until later.

Make it a point to develop positive thinking as quickly as possible. It will speed results. Begin disciplining your thinking in other ways and changing some of your adverse character traits, such as developing decisiveness. Quite a number of minor matters should be dealt with before approaching anything of major importance. The reason for beginning with minor conditions is that they are easier to correct. Success with some of them encourages you and doubts are eased. There will be much less chance of meeting resistances with less important matters.

You may wish to begin breathing exercises at the start of your program. When some minor difficulties have been taken care of, take up more important ones, but continue to avoid the greatest. Then you will be ready for the main ones.

**Arrange a definite schedule.** It is best to arrange a definite schedule for yourself as to the time or hours you will devote to self-betterment. Otherwise you will find yourself putting it off, thinking of other things to do which may seem more important at the moment. This may be a way of unconsciously avoiding coming to grips with unpleasant problems. Even if you decide to devote only one or two hours a week to this work, schedule the time and stick to it. You will be developing a habit pattern.

In your program you should be using the technique of ideomotor replies to questions in order to learn the sources and causes of your individual problems. Keep the seven usual factors in mind. Some apply to other conditions as well as to illnesses. List the seven and refer to them continually so you do not overlook some additional cause involved in a particular matter.

If several reasons are present, you may find no change in the symptom until all have been uncovered. Then go over them in your mind and tell your subconscious also to review the situation. Suggest that it change its viewpoint, if that is necessary, and that it relieve the symptom or condition. In this way you are prodding it to digest the knowledge.

You will find the questioning technique to be a fascinating and very interesting phenomenon. Before trying to set up your four movements in replying, explain it to someone else and let him hold the pendulum while you ask for the movements for *yes*, *no*, etc. Seeing how it moves for someone else will make it easier to establish your own movements. Set up pendulum replies before trying to have your fingers move to reply to questions, as this will come easier then.

In addition to the questioning technique, take a half-hour at least to attempt automatic writing. Many will succeed in this and it is an advantage since the subconscious is not limited to affirmative and negative replies. It can even advance information when writing automatically.

**Never overlook safeguards.** Do not overlook the safeguards of asking if it is all right for you to learn about some particular matter, or all right to recall some event.

When you return to some past experience in your memory, you may tend to partially age regress, whether or not you are in hypnosis. After going over the event again and again, be sure to bring yourself back to the present time.

You would come back spontaneously, but might find some of the emotions tied to the experience persisting and upsetting you. Returning to the present time is accomplished merely by suggesting it. "Now I am coming back to the present, back to—" (naming the day and date). During such recall, if any emotion becomes too strong and you are very fearful, you can end the regression in this way. It is most unlikely for such a situation to happen. If something is too frightening or unpleasant to tolerate, your subconscious would never let you reach it.

Becoming interested in hypnosis you may be tempted to try to hypnotize someone else. While autohypnosis is perfectly safe, you never know what may be going on in the mind of another and without sufficient knowledge might have something unpleasant happen. This is not very likely, but confine hypnosis to yourself.

As has been pointed out, in illness discretion and commonsense must be used. In addition to any self-therapy, attention from a physician may be highly important.

> *You now have the seven keys with which to unlock the doors to health, happiness and success. Use the keys. "Bon Voyage" in your travels towards your goals. With these methods they can be reached.*

# BOOKS FOR FURTHER READING

Andersen, U. S., *Three Magic Words*. New York: Thomas Nelson and Sons, 1955.

Ambrose, *Hypnotherapy with Children*. London: Staples Press, 1961.

August, R., *Hypnosis in Obstetrics*. New York: McGraw-Hill Book Company, Inc., 1961.

Baudouin, C., *Suggestion and Autosuggestion*. New York: Dodd, Mead & Co., 1922.

Bristol, C., *The Magic of Believing*. Englewood Cliffs, N.J.: Prentice-Hall, Inc., 1957.

Caprio, F. S. and Berger, J. R., *Helping Yourself with Self-Hypnosis*. Englewood Cliffs, N.J.: Prentice-Hall, Inc., 1963.

Cooke, C. E. and VanVogt, A. E., *Hypnotism Handbook*. Los Angeles: Borden Publishing Co., 1957.

Dunlap, K., *Habits, Their Making and Unmaking*. New York: Liveright Publishing Co., 1951.

Estabrooks, G., *Hypnotism*. New York: E. P. Dutton & Co., Inc., 1957.

Gutheil, E. A., *Handbook of Dream Analysis*. New York: Liveright Publishing Co., 1951.

Fodor, N., *New Approaches to Dream Interpretation*. New York: Citadel Press, 1951.

Hart, H., *Autoconditioning* (Life). Englewood Cliffs, N.J.: Prentice-Hall, Inc., 1956.

Heise, J., *The Amazing Hypno-Diet*. New York: Belmont Productions, 1962.

207

King, A., *The Cigarette Habit*. Garden City, New York: Doubleday & Co., Inc., 1959.

Kroger, W., *Clinical and Experimental Hypnosis*. New York: J. B. Lippincott Co., 1963.

LeCron, L. M. and Bordeaux, J., *Hypnotism Today*. New York: Grune & Stratton, Inc., 1947.

LeCron, L. M., ed., *Experimental Hypnosis*. New York: The Macmillan Company, 1952.

LeCron, L. M., *Techniques of Hypnotherapy*. New York: Julian Press, 1962.

Long, M. F., *Self-Suggestion*. Vista, California, 1958.

Maltz, M., *Psycho-Cybernetics*. Englewood Cliffs, N.J.: Prentice-Hall, Inc., 1960.

Peale, N. V., *The Power of Positive Thinking*. Englewood Cliffs, N.J.: Prentice-Hall, Inc., 1952.

Powers, M. A., *A Practical Guide to Self-Hypnosis*. Hollywood: Wilshire Book Co., 1961.

Prince, M., *The Unconscious*. New York: The Macmillan Co., 1929.

Weitzenhoffer, O. G., *General Techniques of Hypnotism*. New York: Grune & Stratton, Inc., 1957.

Winters, L., *Origins of Illness and Anxiety*. New York: Julian Press, 1962.

Wolberg, L., *Medical Hypnosis*. New York: Grune & Stratton, Inc., 1948.